D0514242

THE REALLY USEFUL
ULTIMATE
STUDENT
CURRY
COOK
BOOK

MURDOCH BOOKS

Published by Murdoch Books Pty Limited

Murdoch Books Australia
Pier 8/9, 23 Hickson Road, Millers Point NSW 2000
Phone: +61 (0) 2 8220 2000   Fax: +61 (0) 2 8220 2558

Murdoch Books UK Limited
Erico House, 6th Floor, 93-99 Upper Richmond Road
Putney, London SW15 2TG
Phone: +44 (0) 20 8785 5995   Fax: + 44 (0) 20 8785 5985

Chief Executive: Juliet Rogers
Publishing Director: Kay Scarlett

Publisher: Lynn Lewis
Designers: Heather Menzies and Clare O'Loughlin
Project Editor: Zoe Harpham
Editorial Coordinator: Liz Malcolm
Production: Joan Beal

Printed in China in 2010

ISBN 978 1 74196 762 3

RECIPE NOTES

🔘 Degree of difficulty

🔘 Approximate time required to prepare and cook each recipe

🔘 Indicates serving size

🔘 Indicates dishes that are suitable for vegetarians

IMPORTANT: Those who might be at risk from the effects of salmonella poisoning
(the elderly, pregnant women, young children and those suffering from immune deficiency
diseases) should consult their doctor with any concerns about eating raw eggs.

CONVERSION GUIDE: You may find cooking times vary depending on the oven you
are using. For fan-forced ovens, as a general rule, set the oven temperature to 20°C
(70°F) lower than indicated in the recipe. We have used 20 ml (4 teaspoon) tablespoon
measures. If you are using a 15 ml (3 teaspoon) tablespoon, for most recipes the
difference will not be noticeable. However, for recipes using baking powder, gelatine,
bicarbonate of soda, small amounts of flour and cornflour (cornstarch), add an extra
teaspoon for each tablespoon specified.

CONTENTS

INTRODUCTION

Traditionally, curry was eaten in India and South East Asia, but its popularity has grown in recent decades and it has become a vital part of international cuisine, enjoyed all over the world. Each country has its own interpretation of curried dishes built on local ingredients and culinary traditions. Not all curries are fiery hot with chillies — a popular misconception. This book is filled with recipes ranging from hot and spicy Indian curries and sweet and creamy Thai curries, to milder vegetarian and seafood options — something to suit every taste and mood.

It's well known that curries are packed with flavour, but they're also healthy and even better, simple to cook. If you're new to cooking, you'll find yourself able to master the art of creating the perfect curry in very little time. It's an ideal dish if you're a student because it can be left to cook for a few hours while you study, or prepared in advance and frozen, then reheated when you need a quick meal. It's also a great dish to share with a group of friends at the end of a long day. Serve it with some of the side dishes and accompaniments featured in this book, such as cucumber raita or naan bread, and it's sure to be a winner.

Before you begin cooking, it's worthwhile stocking your cupboards with some of the essential ingredients and spices you'll need. There's an essential ingredients list on page 14 to help you do just that. Pay a visit to your local Indian or Asian supermarket to investigate what they have on offer, and ask for advice on anything you're unsure of. Keep in mind it's best to buy little and often, because many pre-ground spices will lose their pungency well before their use-by date and fresh produce has a limited lifespan. If you can, buy spices whole and grind them yourself as needed.

As well as plenty of curry recipes, this book has information on the different types of rice available, and how to cook and store them. It also has advice on eating well, with top tips for keeping your diet balanced, and important information on food safety and how to store, prepare, defrost and reheat your food correctly.

Armed with all this knowledge, and some fantastic recipes, you'll not only be on the path to creating delicious curries, but a healthy, balanced lifestyle that will help you keep on top of your studies. Happy cooking!

EATING WELL

Eating well is the key to getting the best from life. If you plan to cram your revision or study late into the night, it is essential that you eat a well-balanced diet that will not only keep your mind and body fuelled, but can also help prevent heart disease, tooth decay and obesity as well as many other common illnesses. Studies have shown, for example, that you're less likely to get a cold if you have a good intake of vitamin C, which is something to think about if you've got exams or a heavy workload looming.

Generally speaking, the more varied your diet, the more likely it is that all the vital nutrients you need are being provided. In order to ensure you are getting enough, you must be eating from each of the three main food groups detailed below. Having discovered how to plan good, balanced meals you should also take a look at the snacks you eat between meals. Try to drink plenty of water and eat yoghurts or fruit if you get hunger pangs – sugary drinks and fried salty snacks will just help you to pile on the weight, and offer very little by way of nutrients.

GROUP 1

CARBOHYDRATES

Starchy foods such as potatoes and bread are good sources of fibre, vitamins and minerals. Carbohydrates like these should be the base of every meal. They are naturally low in fat (and as a nation, we consume far more fat than we need), and will satisfy your hunger.

Your body needs carbohydrates to convert into energy but there are two main types: starch and sugar. When you eat a sugar-filled food or drink, you get an almost instant energy surge, which is quickly followed by a low. Your brain tells you that you need more energy and you crave another bar of chocolate or can of fizzy pop. Yo-yoing energy levels can leave you feeling lethargic and unable to concentrate on your studies. Because starches are digested by the body far more slowly than sugars, they give a constant slow-releasing source of energy which is exactly what you need if you're going into a three-hour exam. If you have a heavy day ahead, you must eat a proper breakfast. When you wake up, your sugar levels are low so boost them up with sustaining food. Have a couple of slices of toast and Marmite or a good quality-fruit preserve and a big bowl of muesli or porridge. Avoid tea or coffee and have a glass of fresh orange juice instead.

At meal times, go for filled baked potatoes, risottos, stews, curries and pair stir-fries, soups or salads with a carbohydrate for a healthy, well-balanced meal.

Good carbohydrates include:

rice and grains

----

pulses: lentils, beans and dried peas

----

breakfast cereals: muesli, porridge and wheat blocks, not sugar coated cereals

----

bread: wholemeal is best but white is still good

----

pasta

----

potatoes

----

noodles

GROUP 2

PROTEIN

The body needs protein for the production of body tissue, so to keep strong and healthy, it must be included in your diet. Most people easily consume enough protein so it is not something that you really need to worry about, but it is worth keeping an eye on if you are vegetarian, constantly dieting, or on a very limited budget for food. You don't need to consume a lot, but you should make an effort to include a small amount with each meal. Unfortunately, a lot of high protein food is also high in fat, so choose lean meat and trim off any fat, and be aware of how much cheese, cream and butter you eat.

The type and quality of protein varies greatly in different foods. Animal proteins such as fish, milk and poultry are the most complete, but there are plenty of good, but not quite as complex plant sources of protein to be found in carbohydrates such as grains, pulses, beans and potatoes. The best way to ensure quality, not just quantity, is to try and combine proteins so they complement each other. This is particularly important if you're vegetarian and even more so for vegans who don't eat dairy produce. Try and eat at least two different foods together to obtain a high quality protein; fortunately this is the way that most foods go together anyway – a good example is baked beans on toast which is a very good high fibre, high protein, low-fat snack meal.

Quality high protein foods include:

- fish and shellfish • lean meat • poultry • milk • yoghurt

- cheese • eggs • butter • tofu • nuts • seeds • peanut butter

- seaweed • grains • beans • cereals • pasta

GROUP 3

FRUIT & VEGETABLES

The World Health Organisation recommends that we eat at least 400g, that's almost a pound, or five portions of fruit and vegetables a day – that doesn't include potatoes but does include beans, nuts and seeds. Fruit and vegetables are packed with different vitamins and minerals, so you should try and vary the types you eat and remember that it's impossible to eat too much. Choose fresh or dried fruit in preference to a bar of chocolate or crisps.

The way that you cook the vegetables is of the utmost importance, as it is very easy to destroy the nutrients. Leafy greens are packed with water-soluble vitamin C, so the traditional method of boiling them in water means that when you eat the vegetables, you may still get the fibre but the nutrients and most of the flavour have gone down the drain. Instead, try stir-frying, steaming or cooking methods which involve eating the liquid that the vegetables have been cooked in, such as soups, stews and pasta sauces.

As soon as they are harvested, fruit and green vegetables begin to deteriorate nutritionally. Don't store them for weeks, but eat within a few days of buying. Frozen and canned vegetables are just as good, and in some cases better than fresh. Take frozen spinach for example, which is picked, prepared and quickly frozen within hours, locking in a good percentage of the nutrients.

TOP TIPS FOR EATING WELL

- Base your meals on starchy carbohydrates to get a constant supply of energy.

- Cut back on sugary snacks – don't satisfy your hunger with empty kilojoules that leave you craving more.

- Try to avoid stimulants such as chocolate, cola and coffee – keep your mind and body on an even keel.

- Ensure you get enough high quality protein – try and eat at least two together. If you are vegetarian, don't base your diet on dairy produce – eat plenty of nuts and pulses.

- Keep an eye on your fat intake, including butter, cream and cheese.

- Try to eat five portions of fruit and vegetables each day – take care when preparing and cooking vegetables; don't destroy their vitamin content.

FOOD SAFETY

The most important thing to remember when you're responsible for feeding yourself, is to keep the kitchen clean. It isn't all that difficult to give yourself (or your house-mates) food poisoning, but if you cook your food carefully and observe basic hygiene and storage rules, you won't put anybody's health at risk.

Here are a few pointers that you should keep in mind:

• Keep the kitchen floor clean; don't encourage mice, rats and other vermin to set up home in your house.

• Don't let dirty pots pile up or bacteria will multiply at an astonishing rate, making your kitchen unsafe and smelly. While you're cooking, try and wash-up as you go and wash the used plates and cutlery straight after you've eaten.

• Wash up in very hot, soapy water. Use rubber gloves and a scrubbing brush and take care to rinse the dishes well with clean hot water.

• Leave the washing-up to air-dry on the draining board – dirty tea towels will just spread germs onto a clean plate, so make sure they're laundered regularly.

Clean up splashes and spillages immediately after they occur as they make the floor dangerously slippery and can become ingrained and harbour bacteria. Bits of food on the floor and under the cooker can also encourage the odd mouse or two to set up home in your kitchen.

Wash your hands before you start cooking.

Keep the fridge clean. It's easy to forget a small lump of cheese that's left to go green at the back of the fridge, if it's not cleaned out regularly. Mould quickly spreads from bad food to healthy like the one bad apple in the sack. It's not only risky but costly.

Never keep food past its use-by date.

If a chilled item has been left out of the fridge and has become warm, play safe and throw it away, especially if it's made from dairy produce.

Store raw meat properly wrapped up and well away from cooked foods. It is better to keep raw meat at the bottom of the fridge so that there's no danger of blood dripping down onto cooked food.

Use a separate chopping board for raw meat as contamination (particularly from pork and poultry) to other foods is common. Scrub boards thoroughly after use.

Wash your hands thoroughly after touching meat. Take care not to touch pan handles, knives or tea towels while preparing raw meat and before you have washed

- Store dry goods in a cool, dark place. Keep bags sealed with tape and check use-by dates.

- Take chilled or frozen food home as quickly as possible and store at the correct temperature. Don't refreeze food that has already been defrosted.

- Take care when defrosting food especially meat, fish and poultry. Never force food to defrost quickly but leave it wrapped up at room temperature or even better, in the fridge until completely thawed. Don't ever be tempted by helpful friends who suggest 'rinsing the frozen prawns under the hot tap', or 'leaving the chicken in the sink full of hot water. Such methods are likely to result in food poisoning.

- Don't reheat food more than once.

ESSENTIAL CURRY INGREDIENTS

If you've only got half a cupboard and a shelf in the fridge to store your curry provisions, then you're going to have to think carefully about what you buy, or you'll end up wasting a lot of space.

Here's a list of all the things you ought to have in store. Apart from the items listed below, buy fresh produce and specific ingredients as required.

CUPBOARD

ESSENTIALS

• packet of rice (whatever type you prefer)

• can of chopped tomatoes

• small bottle of olive oil

• small bottle of vegetable oil

• small bottle of vinegar

• small tub of curry powder and/or jar of curry paste

• small tub of chilli powder

- small jar of turmeric
- small jar of cumin seeds
- small jar of fenugreek seeds
- small jar of cardomom seeds
- small jar of coriander seeds
- small jar of dried chillies
- garlic
- salt and pepper

NOT ESSENTIAL, BUT VERY HANDY

- small tin of coconut cream
- palm sugar (jaggery) or soft brown sugar
- packet of frozen peas
- shrimp paste
- curry leaves
- mustard powder

- packet of poppadoms

- flour

- beef, chicken or vegetable stock cubes or liquid stock

FREEZER

If you have space in a freezer, then you can freeze portions of meat, poultry and fish for later use. Make sure you follow the food safety tips on page 13 when defrosting and reheating.

FRIDGE

There are very few chilled items that are real essentials; most of them are perishable and need to be bought as needed. The list below contains items that should be bought once you've decided on a specific curry to cook, as close to the day of cooking as possible. We have included fresh herbs in the list, but why not have a go at growing your own – a small pot from the supermarket is not too pricey and with a bit of love and attention, will survive happily on a sunny windowsill.

BUY AS NEEDED

- tub of plain yoghurt

- onions

- carrots

- potatoes
- pumpkin
- aubergine (eggplant)
- cucumber
- green beans
- lemons
- limes
- beef
- lamb
- pork
- poultry
- fish and prawns
- lemongrass
- red and green chillies
- Thai basil
- coriander
- mint

RICE AND COOKING METHODS

Rice is eaten daily by millions of people worldwide. Nearly half of the world's population relies on it as a staple food, though its popularity across the globe is by no means evenly spread—Asia produces almost 90 per cent of the rice in the world, but consumes most of it as well.

BUYING RICE

Only a few years ago, the supermarket would have stocked two, maybe three, types of rice—long-grain, short-grain and perhaps brown. What a difference a few years make. Today, supermarkets stock enough varieties of rice to cover most of the basic uses. They will generally have arborio, which is a good rice for risottos and a fine stand-in for paella rice; fragrant jasmine rice, which is perfect for Southeast Asian dishes; basmati for pilaffs and to serve with Indian meals; as well as short-grain, long-grain and brown rice. Most will also include some wild rice, but you may have to venture to a healthfood store if your supermarket cannot help. If you want something a bit more specific, try ethnic grocery stores. They often have a wider selection, in larger quantities, at a cheaper price.

STORING RICE

If you eat a lot of rice, buy it in large quantities—it has a long shelf life and an unopened packet can be kept for several years without loss of quality. Once you have opened a fresh packet of rice, store it in a cool, dark, dry place in an airtight container. Rice bought in large sacks is best transferred to a dry, clean container with a lid.

Brown rice is an exception. Because it still contains the oil-rich germ or bran layer, it has a higher fat content than milled, or white, rice, and goes rancid if left in a warm place for too long. For this reason, it is best stored in an airtight container in the fridge.

You also need to take extra care with cooked rice. If it is not consumed immediately, cover it, then chill it quickly as harmful bacteria can grow rapidly. Cooked rice will store in the fridge for up to 2 days only.

COOKING RICE

One of the best things about rice is that it needs very little attention. Give it a quick rinse and then put it on to cook while you focus on the rest of the meal. There are several methods of cooking rice, all with good results. Experiment with each method and work out your favourite, then get cooking.

CLEANING

Traditionally, rice had to be picked over and any stones or grit discarded. Most modern-day rice is clean enough that it does not require checking, though rice bought in sacks may still need picking over.

Once upon a time, all rice was washed prior to cooking. Today, personal preference dictates whether this is done or not—most rices sold commercially are clean enough that this step can be omitted. Many cooks in Asia often both wash their rice and soak it to shorten the cooking time. One point to remember—if you do wash or soak your rice before cooking it, remember to drain it thoroughly, particularly when cooking by the absorption method, or you will have too much liquid to cook the rice properly.

COOKING
Rice can be cooked in a number of different ways. Some rices will lend themselves to being cooked using more than one method, but others suit just one method. Individual recipes will guide you.

If reheating cooked rice, make sure all the rice is piping hot to destroy any bacteria that may be present.

ABSORPTION METHOD
Probably the most familiar method of cooking rice, the absorption method is an efficient and nutritious way to cook rice, as nutrients are not discarded with the cooking water. Generally, long-grain rices suit this method. A measured amount of rice is cooked in a measured amount of water so that all the water is absorbed. To cook, put the rice in cold water, then bring to the boil, cover with a tight-fitting lid, then reduce the heat to a simmer so that the rice at the bottom of the pan doesn't burn. The rice is cooked by the hot water and by the remaining steam once the water has been absorbed. Once cooked, simply fluff up with a fork and serve immediately.

The electric rice cooker is designed to cook rice the absorption way. Sold in Asian stores, many kitchen stores and some department stores, they have markings on the inside to show the amount of water needed for the amount of rice. It automatically switches off when the grains are cooked, so the rice is then steam-dried. Usually, though, it is only the portion closer to the surface which is steamed—the rice at the bottom of the cooker is boiled. The rice cooker then keeps the rice warm until you're ready to eat it. A general rule of thumb when cooking by the absorption method is to make sure that the depth of uncooked rice in the pan, pot or

electric rice cooker is no more than 5 cm (2 inches) high, or the
rice will cook unevenly.

RAPID BOILING

Like pasta, many rices, from arborio to parboiled rices, cook well
in plenty of water. Bring a large saucepan of water to the boil,
uncovered. Sprinkle in the rice and keep an eye on it, so it does not
stick or overcook. Drain the rice in a sieve (if you are using jasmine
or Japanese rice, rinse it with a little tepid water to prevent it
cooking further).

STEAMING RICE

This method is preferred for sticky rice. Soak the rice overnight,
then drain. Spread out the grains in a steamer, and put the
steamer over a wok or pan of boiling water. The rice does not
touch the water—it is cooked only by the steam.

LEFTOVERS

If you have any leftover rice, don't throw it away—most cultures
have developed recipes specifically to use up leftover rice, from
Italian arancini to use up leftover risotto, and fried rice in China
and Southeast Asia, to sticky rice crackers in Thailand. Once the
cooked rice has cooled, store it in an airtight container in the
refrigerator, and eat within 2 days — you must heat it thoroughly
before eating.

BASICS

SPICE PASTES AND POWDERS

To get the best out of a curry, you need to start with the basics —a rich, fragrant curry paste. You'll really notice the difference between a home-made curry paste and a bought one but, when time is tight, there are many good commercial curry pastes available.

One of the best accompaniments to a curry is a steaming bowl of freshly cooked rice. You can choose simple steamed rice or jazz it up a little with some simple flavourings that complement the curry. Basmati rice is the traditional accompaniment to Indian meals while Southeast Asian curries more often come with jasmine rice.

BALTI MASALA PASTE

This paste makes more than you'll need for one meal; store the remainder in a clean, airtight container in the fridge for up to 1 month.

Dry-fry cinnamon sticks, coriander seeds, cumin seeds, black mustard seeds, cardamom seeds, fenugreek seeds, fennel seeds and the cloves in a small frying pan seperately over medium heat for 2–3 minutes, or until each of the spices just starts to become fragrant.

Transfer all the spices to a food processor or mortar and pestle, allow to cool and process or grind to a powder. Add the bay leaves, curry leaves, ground turmeric, garlic, ginger, chilli powder and 185 ml (6 fl oz/³⁄₄ cup) vinegar, and combine well.

Heat the oil in the pan, add the paste and cook, stirring, for 5 minutes. Stir in remaining vinegar.

4 tablespoons coriander seeds

2 tablespoons cumin seeds

2 cinnamon sticks, crumbled

2 teaspoons fennel seeds

2 teaspoons black mustard seeds

2 teaspoons cardamom seeds

1 teaspoon fenugreek seeds

6 cloves

4 bay leaves

20 curry leaves

1 tablespoon ground turmeric

2 garlic cloves, crushed

1 tablespoon grated ginger

1¹⁄₂ teaspoons chilli powder

250 ml (9 fl oz/1 cup) malt vinegar

125 ml (4 fl oz/¹⁄₂ cup) oil

CHU CHEE CURRY PASTE

10 large dried red chillies

1 teaspoon coriander seeds

1 tablespoon shrimp paste (wrapped in foil)

1 tablespoon white peppercorns

10 kaffir lime (makrut) leaves, finely shredded

10 red Asian shallots, chopped

2 teaspoons finely grated kaffir lime (makrut) rind

1 tablespoon chopped coriander (cilantro) stem and root

1 lemongrass stem, white part only, finely chopped

3 tablespoons chopped fresh galangal

1 tablespoon chopped krachai, optional

6 garlic cloves, chopped

lemon juice, optional

This paste uses krachai (bottled lesser galangal), which is available from Asian grocery stores. It can be omitted, though, if you can't find it. You probably won't need to use all of this paste for one meal; store the rest in a clean, airtight container for up to 1 month in the fridge.

Preheat the oven to 180°C (350°F/Gas 4). Soak the chillies in boiling water for 10 minutes. Drain, remove the seeds and roughly chop.

Place the coriander seeds, shrimp paste and peppercorns on a foil-lined baking tray, and bake for 5 minutes, or until fragrant. Remove the foil.

Place all the ingredients in a food processor or mortar and pestle. Process or grind to a smooth paste. You may need to add a little lemon juice if the paste is too thick.

REALLY EASY!

25 MINUTES + SOAKING TIME

MAKES 1/2 CUP

GREEN CURRY PASTE

This recipe is for a large batch, so store the rest in a clean, airtight container for up to 2 weeks in the fridge or 2 months in the freezer.

Place the coriander and cumin seeds in a dry frying pan and toast over medium heat for 2–3 minutes, shaking the pan constantly.

Pound the roasted spices and peppercorns in a mortar and pestle until finely ground.

Wrap the shrimp paste in a small piece of foil and cook under a hot grill (broiler) for 3 minutes, turning the package twice.

Place the ground spices and the shrimp paste in a food processor and then process for 5 seconds. Add the remaining ingredients and 2 tablespoons of salt and process for 20 seconds at a time, scraping down the sides of the processor bowl with a spatula each time, until a smooth paste is formed.

1 tablespoon coriander seeds

2 teaspoons cumin seeds

1 teaspoon black peppercorns

2 teaspoons shrimp paste

8 large green chillies, roughly chopped

20 red Asian shallots

5 cm (2 inch) piece galangal, chopped

12 small garlic cloves, chopped

50 g (1¾ oz/ 1 cup) chopped coriander (cilantro) leaves, stems and roots

6 kaffir lime (makrut) leaves, chopped

3 lemongrass stems, white part only, finely chopped

2 teaspoons grated lime zest

2 tablespoons oil

REALLY EASY! · 30 MINUTES · MAKES 1 CUP

MADRAS CURRY PASTE

2¹/₂ tablespoons coriander
seeds, dry-roasted and
ground

1 tablespoon cumin seeds,
dry-roasted and ground

1 teaspoon brown mustard
seeds

¹/₂ teaspoon cracked black
peppercorns

1 teaspoon chilli powder

1 teaspoon ground
turmeric

2 garlic cloves, crushed

2 teaspoons grated ginger

3–4 tablespoons white
vinegar

If this is one of your favourite pastes, make two
batches and store in a clean, airtight container in
the fridge for 2 weeks or the freezer for 2 months.

Place ground coriander, ground cumin, mustard
seeds, cracked black peppercorns, chilli powder,
ground turmeric, garlic, ginger and 1 teaspoon salt
in a small bowl, and combine well. Add the vinegar
and mix to a smooth paste.

REALLY EASY!   5 MINUTES   MAKES ¹/₂ CUP

MUSAMAN CURRY PASTE

This recipe makes more paste than you'll need, so store any leftover paste in a clean, airtight container. It will last for at least 2 weeks in the fridge and for 2 months in a freezer.

Place the coriander, cumin and cardamom seeds in a dry frying pan. Roast over medium heat for about 2 minutes, shaking the pan continuously.

Put the roasted spices and peppercorns in a mortar and pestle and pound until finely ground.

Place the ground spices and remaining ingredients in a food processor. Process for 20 seconds and scrape down the sides of the bowl with a spatula. Continue processing for 5 seconds at a time, wiping down the sides of the bowl between processing, until a smooth paste is formed.

1 tablespoon coriander seeds

1 tablespoon cumin seeds

seeds from 4 cardamom pods

2 teaspoons black peppercorns

1 tablespoon shrimp paste

1 teaspoon ground nutmeg

$1/2$ teaspoon ground cloves

15 dried red chillies

10 red Asian shallots, chopped

2 lemongrass stems, white part only, finely chopped

6 small garlic cloves, chopped

1 tablespoon oil

PENANG CURRY PASTE

2 dried long red chillies, about 13 cm (5 inches) long

----

2 lemongrass stems, white part only, thinly sliced

2.5 cm (1 inch) piece galangal, finely chopped

4–5 garlic cloves, finely chopped

3–4 red Asian shallots, finely chopped

5–6 coriander (cilantro) roots, finely chopped

----

1 teaspoon shrimp paste

----

1 teaspoon ground cumin, dry-roasted

----

3 tablespoons peanuts, chopped

----

vegetable oil, as needed

If you don't like the idea of bashing the ingredients together with a mortar and pestle, you can use a small food processor or blender to blend them into as smooth a paste as possible. Add vegetable oil, as required, to assist with the blending.

Remove the stems from the chillies and slit them lengthways with a sharp knife. Discard the seeds and soak the chillies in hot water for 1–2 minutes or until soft. Drain and roughly chop.

Using a mortar and pestle, pound the chillies, lemongrass and galangal into a paste. Add the remaining ingredients one at a time and pound until the mixture forms a very smooth paste.

EASY!   15 MINUTES   MAKES 1/3 CUP

RED CURRY PASTE

The reason the shrimp paste is enclosed in a piece of foil is to prevent it stinking out your kitchen — shrimp paste has a very powerful odour.

Place the coriander and cumin seeds in a dry frying pan and roast over medium heat for 2–3 minutes, shaking the pan constantly.

Place the roasted spices and peppercorns in a mortar and pestle and pound until finely ground.

Wrap the shrimp paste in a small piece of foil and cook under a hot grill (broiler) for 3 minutes, turning the package twice.

Place ground spices, shrimp paste, nutmeg and chilli in a food processor; process for 5 seconds. Add the remaining ingredients and 2 teaspoons salt and process for 20 seconds at a time, scraping down the sides of the processor bowl each time, until a smooth paste is formed.

EASY! · 30 MINUTES · MAKES 1 CUP

1 tablespoon coriander seeds

2 teaspoons cumin seeds

1 teaspoon black peppercorns

2 teaspoons shrimp paste

1 teaspoon ground nutmeg

12 dried or fresh red chillies, roughly chopped

20 red Asian shallots, chopped

2 tablespoons oil

4 lemongrass stems, white part only, finely chopped

12 small garlic cloves, chopped

4 tablespoons coriander (cilantro) stems and roots, chopped

6 kaffir lime (makrut) leaves, chopped

2 teaspoons grated lime zest

2 teaspoons ground turmeric

1 teaspoon paprika

SAMBAL OELEK

12 large dried red chillies

2 large red onions, roughly chopped

6 garlic cloves

1 teaspoon shrimp paste

125 ml (4 fl oz/$\frac{1}{2}$ cup) oil

$\frac{3}{4}$ cup (185 ml/6 fl oz) tamarind concentrate

1 tablespoon shaved palm sugar (jaggery), or soft brown sugar

1 teaspoon ground pepper

This is a very hot paste, so take care and use it sparingly! It is used as a relish in Indonesian and Malaysian cooking and can also be a substitute for fresh chillies in most recipes. This recipe makes enough to keep you going for a few months. Store excess paste in a clean, airtight container in the refrigerator for up to 2 weeks or freeze for up to 3 months — wait until it is cool before pouring the paste into a jar.

Soak the dried red chillies in hot water for around 30 minutes; drain.

Place the chillies, onions, garlic, shrimp paste and oil in a food processor and mix into a smooth paste, scraping down the sides regularly.

Heat a heavy-based pan over low heat and cook the paste for 10 minutes, stirring regularly, until very oily. Stir in the tamarind concentrate, sugar, ground pepper and 2 teaspoons salt. Bring to the boil and simmer for 2 minutes.

EASY! · 20 MINUTES + SOAKING TIME · MAKES 1 CUP

VINDALOO PASTE

This paste will keep for up to 1 month in a clean, airtight container.

Place all the ingredients in a food processor and process for 20 seconds, or until all the ingredients are well combined and smooth.

2 tablespoons grated ginger

4 garlic cloves, chopped

4 red chillies, chopped

2 teaspoons ground turmeric

2 teaspoons ground cardamom

4 whole cloves

6 peppercorns

1 teaspoon ground cinnamon

1 tablespoon ground coriander

1 tablespoon cumin seeds

125 ml (4 fl oz/$^{1}/_{2}$ cup) cider vinegar

YELLOW CURRY PASTE

8 small green chillies

5 red Asian shallots, roughly chopped

2 garlic cloves, chopped

1 tablespoon finely chopped coriander (cilantro) roots and stems

1 lemongrass stem, white part only, chopped

2 tablespoons finely chopped galangal

1 teaspoon ground coriander

1 teaspoon ground cumin

1/2 teaspoon ground turmeric

1/2 teaspoon black peppercorns

1 tablespoon lime juice

This is a really useful paste to keep in the fridge for a quick dinner — it will keep for up to 1 month in a clean, airtight container. Fry some onion and sliced chicken or beef in oil, add 3–4 tablespoons of this paste and 250 ml (9 fl oz/1 cup) coconut milk and simmer for 15 minutes before adding some chopped green vegetables and cooking them until they are tender.

Place all the ingredients in a food processor, blender or mortar and pestle and process or grind to a smooth paste.

REALLY EASY!   20 MINUTES   MAKES 1/2 CUP

CHAAT MASALA

Chaat masala is a salty, tangy seasoning used in popular Indian snacks such as bhel puri, a puffed rice dish. Toss it through dry snack mixes or sprinkle it onto fruit and vegetables as a seasoning.

Place a small frying pan over low heat and dry-roast the coriander seeds until aromatic. Remove from the pan and dry-roast the cumin seeds, then separately, the ajowan. Grind the roasted mixture to a fine powder with the other ingredients, using a spice grinder or mortar and pestle. Store in an airtight container.

Notes: Ajowan is a spice that looks like miniature cumin seeds and has a similar aroma but stronger flavour. Black salt has a sulfuric flavour that is an acquired taste. It is more pinky-tan than black in colour. Amchoor powder is a fine beige powder which is made by drying green mangoes. All three are available at Indian food stores.

4 tablespoons coriander seeds

2 tablespoons cumin seeds

1 teaspoon ajowan

3 tablespoons black salt

1 tablespoon amchoor powder

2 dried chillies

1 teaspoon black peppercorns

1 teaspoon pomegranate seeds

REALLY EASY! · 10 MINUTES · MAKES 10 TABLESPOONS

8 cardamom pods

2 Indian bay leaves (cassia leaves)

1 teaspoon black peppercorns

2 teaspoons cumin seeds

2 teaspoons coriander seeds

5 cm (2 inch) cinnamon stick

1 teaspoon cloves

This a northern Indian spice mix, the name of which means 'warming spice mix'. There are many commercial versions available if you'd prefer to buy one, rather than make your own. Keep in a small airtight container for about a month.

Remove the seeds from the cardamom pods. Break the bay leaves into small pieces. Put them in a spice grinder or mortar and pestle with the remaining spices and grind to a fine powder. Store in a small airtight container until needed.

REALLY EASY! · 15 MINUTES · MAKES 1/4 CUP

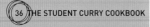

INDIAN CURRY POWDER

There are many versions of Indian curry powder; this one is a basic, general purpose one. It will keep for a month or so in an airtight container.

Dry-fry the coriander seeds, cumin seeds, mustard seeds and black peppercorns in a large frying pan for 1 minute, or until aromatic. Put in a food processor together with the remaining spices. Process until smooth.

REALLY EASY! 15 MINUTES MAKES 2/3 CUP

3 tablespoons coriander seeds

$1^1/_2$ tablespoons cumin seeds

1 tablespoon black mustard seeds

1 teaspoon black peppercorns

1 tablespoon ground turmeric

2 teaspoons garlic powder

$^1/_2$ teaspoon chilli powder

$^1/_2$ teaspoon ground ginger

PANCH PHORON

1 teaspoon cumin seeds

---

1 teaspoon fennel seeds

---

1 teaspoon fenugreek
seeds

---

1 teaspoon brown mustard
seeds

---

1 teaspoon nigella seeds

Panch phoron is a five-spice mix used to flavour vegetables and pulses. The mix can be fried at the beginning of a dish, or fried and then added as a final seasoning. Store in a small airtight container.

Grind all spices to a fine powder in a spice grinder, in a mortar and pestle, or with a grinding stone

REALLY EASY!

10 MINUTES

MAKES **1** TABLESPOON

SRI LANKAN CURRY POWDER

Use this curry powder in recipes that call for 'Ceylon' or Sri Lankan curry powder. It will keep for a couple of months in an airtight container.

Dry-fry the coriander, cumin, fennel and fenugreek seeds separately over low heat until fragrant. It is important to do this separately, as all spices brown at different rates. Make sure the spices are well browned, not burnt.

Place the browned seeds in a food processor, blender or mortar and pestle, add the remaining ingredients and process or grind to a powder.

3 tablespoons coriander seeds

1 1/2 tablespoons cumin seeds

1 teaspoon fennel seeds

1/4 teaspoon fenugreek seeds

2 cm (3/4 inch) piece cinnamon stick

6 cloves

1/4 teaspoon cardamom seeds

2 teaspoons dried curry leaves

2 small dried red chillies

STEAMED COCONUT RICE

500 g (1 lb 2 oz) long-grain white rice

375 ml (13 fl oz/1½ cups) coconut milk

This is a Malaysian dish and goes well with Malaysian, Indonesian or Singaporean curries.

Pour 500 ml (17 fl oz/2 cups) of water into a wok. Place a large sheet of baking paper in the base of a large bamboo steamer and spread the rice in the base of the steamer. Bring the water to the boil, sit the steamer over the wok (it should not touch the water) and put the lid on the steamer. Steam the rice for 35 minutes, turning the rice over halfway through cooking time, and replenishing the water, if necessary.

Gently heat the coconut milk, with 1 teaspoon salt, in a saucepan. Add the steamed rice, bring to the boil and stir well. Cover with a tight-fitting lid and remove from the heat. Set aside for 45 minutes, or until the coconut milk is absorbed.

Spread the rice back into the paper-lined steaming bamboo basket and cover. Check that there is water in the wok, add more if needed, then steam for another 30 minutes.

EASY!

1¼ HOURS + STANDING TIME

SERVES 4

STEAMED FRAGRANT RICE

This is a basic recipe for steamed rice. You can adjust the flavourings to suit the recipe you are serving it with.

Wash the rice in a sieve until the water runs clear. In a large saucepan, fry the garlic cloves and ginger in the oil, ghee or butter.

Add 750 ml (26 fl oz/3 cups) water, bring to the boil and cook for 1 minute. Cover with a tight-fitting lid, reduce the heat to as low as possible and cook for 10–15 minutes or until steam tunnels form on the surface and the rice is soft and swollen.

Turn off the heat and leave the pan, covered, for about 10 minutes. Fluff with a fork.

500 g (1 lb 2 oz/2$^{1}/_{2}$ cups) long-grain white rice

1–2 garlic cloves, crushed

2 tablespoons finely grated ginger

2 tablespoons oil, ghee or butter

REALLY EASY! · 30 MINUTES · SERVES 6-8

LEMON RICE

300 g (10^1/$_2$ oz/1^1/$_2$ cups) basmati rice

^{3}/$_4$ teaspoon ground turmeric

2 tablespoons desiccated coconut

2 tablespoons milk or coconut milk

2 tablespoons chopped toasted cashews or almonds

4 curry leaves

^{1}/$_3$ teaspoon mustard seeds

^{1}/$_2$–1 green chilli, seeded and chopped

125 g (4^1/$_2$ oz/^{1}/$_2$ cup) ghee

1–2 lemons

The Indian rice basmati is considered the finest rice in the world. It is grown in the foothills of the Himalayas from northern India to Bangladesh. When preparing, pick over the grains before cooking to remove any unhulled grains or sticks.

Wash the rice in a sieve until the water runs clear, then soak in cold water for 15 minutes. Drain well.

Put the rice, 560 ml (19^1/$_4$ fl oz/2^1/$_4$ cups) water and turmeric in a heavy-based saucepan over high heat until boiling. Reduce the heat, cover tightly and cook for 12 minutes.

Moisten the desiccated coconut with milk or coconut milk and set aside. Cook the nuts, curry leaves, mustard seeds and chilli in the ghee until the mustard seeds begin to pop. Stir into the rice and add the coconut and the juice of 1 lemon.

Cover again and cook for 7–8 minutes until the rice has absorbed the liquid and is dry and fluffy. Check for taste, adding extra lemon juice, or serve with the remaining lemon cut into wedges.

REALLY EASY! 30 MINUTES SERVES 4-6

This is a mildly flavoured rice dish, perfect as an accompaniment to Indian or Sri Lankan curries. If you're in a hurry, omit the soaking step.

Wash the rice in a sieve until the water runs clear, then soak in cold water for 15 minutes. Drain well.

Melt the butter gently in a large deep frying pan, add the bay leaves and rice and cook, stirring, for 6 minutes, or until all the moisture has evaporated. Add the saffron and soaking liquid to the rice with the stock and 375 ml (13 fl oz/$1^1/2$ cups) boiling water. Season. Bring to the boil, then reduce the heat to low and cook, covered, for 15 minutes, or until the rice is cooked.

400 g (14 oz/2 cups) basmati rice

25 g (1 oz) butter

3 bay leaves

$1/4$ teaspoon saffron threads, soaked in 2 tablespoons hot water for 2 minutes

500 ml (17 fl oz/2 cups) boiling vegetable stock

BEEF & LAMB

MEAT

The good news about using beef and lamb in curries is that the best cuts to use are the cheapest, so your budget won't suffer. Much like casseroles, meat curries typically cook over a low-medium heat for a long time to allow all the flavours to meld and blend. This long cooking time breaks down the connective tissue of the meat, leaving it tender and juicy .

SRI LANKAN PEPPER BEEF CURRY

Sri Lanka boasts a cuisine that has been influenced by the Indians, Malays, Portuguese, Dutch and British. Its curries are mostly coconut based, and robust with spices. Many, such as this one, are cooked for hours, until the thick, flavoursome sauce clings to the by-now tender main ingredient.

Dry-fry the coriander, cumin and fennel seeds and the black peppercorns in a frying pan over medium–high heat for 2–3 minutes, or until fragrant. Allow to cool. Using a mortar and pestle, or a spice grinder, crush or grind to a powder.

Heat the oil in a heavy-based saucepan over high heat, brown the beef in batches, and set aside. Reduce the heat to medium, add the onion, garlic, ginger, chilli, curry leaves and lemongrass, and cook for 5–6 minutes, or until softened. Add the ground spices and cook for a further 3 minutes.

Put beef back into the pan, and stir well to coat in the spices. Add the lemon juice, coconut milk and beef stock and bring to the boil. Reduce the heat to low, cover and cook for 2$\frac{1}{2}$ hours, or until the beef is very tender and sauce is reduced. While cooking, skim any oil that comes to the surface and discard.

1 tablespoon coriander seeds

2 teaspoons cumin seeds

1 teaspoon fennel seeds

1 tablespoon black peppercorns

3 tablespoons oil

1 kg (2 lb 4 oz) beef chuck steak, diced

2 onions, finely diced

4 garlic cloves, crushed

3 teaspoons finely grated ginger

1 red chilli, seeded, finely chopped

8 curry leaves

1 lemongrass stem, white part only, finely chopped

2 tablespoons lemon juice

250 ml (9 fl oz/1 cup) coconut milk

250 ml (9 fl oz/1 cup) beef stock

EASY! · 3 HOURS · SERVES 6

FRAGRANT DRY BEEF CURRY

CURRY PASTE

2 tablespoons cumin seeds

2 tablespoons coriander seeds

3 green cardamom pods

2 teaspoons white peppercorns

2 teaspoons grated ginger

4 garlic cloves, crushed

2 red onions, roughly chopped

4 long red chillies

2 large handfuls coriander (cilantro) leaves, chopped

3 tablespoons olive oil

1 kg (2 lb 4 oz) beef chuck steak, cut into 2.5 cm (1 inch) pieces

400 g (14 oz) tin chopped tomatoes

2 tablespoons tomato paste (concentrated purée)

300 ml (10½ fl oz) beef stock

200 g (7 oz) plain yoghurt

Serve this curry with basmati rice, naan bread, poppadoms and a scattering of coriander leaves.

Dry-fry the cumin, coriander, cardamom and peppercorns in a frying pan over medium heat until fragrant. Cool and crush using a mortar and pestle or spice grinder.

Blend the curry paste ingredients in a small food processor until a smooth paste forms (add water if required). If you are using a mortar and pestle, remove cardamom pods once seeds are released.

Heat 2 tablespoons of the oil in a large heavy-based saucepan. Brown the beef in batches over medium heat. Remove from the saucepan.

Heat remaining olive oil in the same saucepan and fry curry paste. Stir for 3 minutes, or until fragrant.

Return beef to saucepan and add tomatoes, tomato paste and stock. Reduce heat to low, cover with lid and simmer for 1 hour, stirring occasionally.

Remove saucepan lid, stir and simmer 30 minutes, or until beef is tender and sauce is reduced by half. Season to taste. Stir in yoghurt just before serving.

EASY! 1¾ HOURS SERVES 4

COCONUT BEEF CURRY

This is great served with a flavoured rice, such as steamed coconut rice (page 40). Although this curry takes a long time to cook, the preparation time is short.

Heat the oil in a large saucepan over medium–high heat. Add the onion and cook for 2–3 minutes, or until starting to soften. Add the curry paste and stir for 1 minute, or until fragrant. Add the steak and brown evenly for about 5 minutes.

Pour in the stock and bring to the boil. Reduce the heat to very low and simmer, covered, for 1 hour, or until the meat is tender. Uncover and cook for a further 15 minutes to reduce the sauce.

Add the coconut cream, return to the boil, then simmer over low heat for 15–20 minutes, or until the beef is tender and the sauce has reduced.

2 tablespoons oil

1 large onion, sliced

2 tablespoons vindaloo paste (page 33)

1 kg (2 lb 4 oz) beef chuck steak, trimmed and cubed

250 ml (9 fl oz/1 cup) beef stock

200 ml (7 fl oz) coconut cream

REALLY EASY! 2 HOURS SERVES 4

MEATBALLS WITH PICKLED GARLIC

MEATBALLS

450 g (1 lb) minced (ground) beef

3 garlic cloves, crushed

1 teaspoon white pepper

1 small handful coriander (cilantro) leaves

1 small handful Thai basil

1 spring onion (scallion)

3 teaspoons fish sauce

1 egg

3 tablespoons oil

3 tablespoons green curry paste (page 27)

10cm (4 inch) piece ginger, finely chopped

1 teaspoon turmeric

3 tablespoons fish sauce

3 kaffir lime (makrut) leaves

2 1/2 tablespoons tamarind purée

3 tablespoons chopped pickled garlic

1 1/2 tablespoons shaved palm sugar (jaggery)

This dish involves little preparation, making it a welcome choice when you feel like a curry but can't be bothered with the grinding and roasting. Pickled garlic has a sweet–sour flavour and is used in curries as a means of balancing other flavours, be they hot, creamy or sweet.

Chop the spring onion and herbs finely and then combine with all the other meatball ingredients. Then, taking a tablespoon at a time, roll mixture into small balls. You should have 24 balls.

Heat oil in a heavy-based saucepan over medium heat and add the curry paste, finely chopped ginger and ground turmeric and cook, stirring frequently for about 5 minutes, or until fragrant.

Add the fish sauce, kaffir lime leaves and tamarind. Bring to the boil then cover, reduce to a simmer and cook for 5 minutes. Add the meatballs, pickled garlic and palm sugar and simmer for 15 minutes, or until meatballs are cooked through.

REALLY EASY! | **45** MINUTES | SERVES **4**

MINCED BEEF AND PEA CURRY

This is an interesting way to make a filling, cheap meal using beef mince. Serve with naan (page 245) or pita bread.

Heat the oil in a large saucepan, add the onion and cook, stirring frequently, for 5 minutes, or until lightly golden. Add the garlic, ginger and chilli, and cook for 1 minute, then add the coriander, cumin and turmeric and cook for a further 1 minute.

Add the potato and 125 ml (4 fl oz/^{1}/$_2$ cup) water to the pan, and combine well. Cook, covered, over medium heat for 15 minutes. Add beef and cook, uncovered, stirring frequently, over high heat, for 4–5 minutes, or until it is lightly browned. Break up any lumps with the back of a spoon. Stir in the peas and coconut cream.

Bring to the boil and cook, stirring occasionally, for 10 minutes, or until the curry is almost dry and the peas are cooked through.

2 tablespoons oil

2 onions, chopped

1 garlic clove, finely chopped

1 tablespoon finely chopped ginger

3 large green chillies, seeded, finely chopped

1^1/$_2$ tablespoons ground coriander

1 tablespoon ground cumin

2 teaspoons ground turmeric

750 g (1 lb 10 oz) potatoes, cut into 1.5 cm (^{1}/$_2$ inch) cubes

1.5 kg (3 lb 5 oz) minced (ground) beef

225 g (8 oz) frozen peas

170 ml (5^1/$_2$ fl oz/^{2}/$_3$ cup) coconut cream

EASY! | 1 HOUR | SERVES 6

THAI BASIL AND BEEF

2 tablespoons grated ginger

2 garlic cloves, crushed

500 g (1 lb 2 oz) rump or round steak

250 ml (9 fl oz/1 cup) coconut cream

1 tablespoon yellow curry paste (page 34)

4 tablespoons fish sauce

4 tablespoons shaved palm sugar (jaggery), or soft brown sugar

2 lemongrass stems, white part only, finely chopped

1 thick slice galangal

4 kaffir lime (makrut) leaves

2 tomatoes, cut into 2 cm (³/₄ inch) dice

Continued →

There are two ingredients in this dish that make it distinctly Thai (three if we include the curry paste). The first is Thai basil, with its distinctive aroma and clean flavour and the second is pickled green peppercorns — they add a salty, vinegary, slightly sweet quality, without too much heat.

Crush ginger and garlic to a rough pulp in a mortar with a pestle, or food processor. Cut meat into very thin 5 x 2 cm (2 x ³/₄ inch) strips. Toss the ginger and garlic paste together with the beef and marinate for 30 minutes.

Bring half the coconut cream to the boil in a heavy-based casserole dish over medium heat then reduce to a simmer. Stir in the yellow curry paste and cook for 3–5 minutes. Add the fish sauce and palm sugar and stir until sugar is dissolved.

Increase heat to high, add remaining ingredients, except coconut cream, and 375 ml (13 fl oz/1½ cups) water and bring the curry to the boil then reduce to a simmer and cook uncovered for 1–1¼ hours, or until the beef is tender.

Check seasoning and correct by adding extra fish sauce or palm sugar, if necessary. Stir through the remaining coconut cream and serve immediately.

400 g (14 oz) tinned large bamboo pieces, drained, cut into small chunks

25 g (1 oz) Thai pickled green peppercorns on the stem

2 tablespoons tamarind purée

1 large handful Thai basil, chopped

EASY!   2 HOURS + MARINATING TIME   SERVES 4

BEEF, POTATO AND OKRA CURRY

800 g (1 lb 12 oz) beef chuck steak

2 potatoes

200 g (7 oz) okra

150 g (5$^{1}/_{2}$ oz/1 cup) roughly chopped onion

4 garlic cloves, crushed

3 teaspoons finely chopped ginger

1 teaspoon ground turmeric

$^{1}/_{2}$ teaspoon paprika

$^{1}/_{2}$ teaspoon chilli powder

4 tablespoons oil

1 tablespoon sesame oil

1 teaspoon ground cumin

To make this curry richer in taste, you can use beef stock instead of water. It's great served with lemon wedges and rice.

Cut the beef into 2.5 cm (1 inch) cubes. Peel and cube the potatoes. Trim the okra; if large, halve it lengthways, otherwise leave whole.

Place the onion, garlic, ginger, turmeric, paprika and chilli in a food processor and process until a thick paste is formed.

Heat the oils in a large heavy-based pan. Add the onion mixture and cook over a low heat for about 20 minutes, adding a little water if the mixture starts to stick or burn. When the paste is cooked, it should be a golden brown with oil forming around the edges.

Add the beef and cook, stirring, for 5 minutes, until browned. Add the cumin and combine well. Pour 375 ml (13 fl oz/1$^{1}/_{2}$ cups) water and simmer, covered, for about 2 hours or until the meat is tender. Add potato and okra in the last 45 minutes of cooking; remove the lid for the final 10 minutes until the sauce reduces and thickens. Season with salt to taste.

EASY! · 3 HOURS · SERVES 4

This curry benefits from being made 1 or 2 days in advance to maximise its flavour. Cover with some plastic wrap and store in the fridge until needed. When you're ready to serve, all you need to do is gently reheat it.

Cut the beef into cubes. Heat the ghee or oil in a large pan and cook the onion until just soft.

Add the garlic, chilli, ginger, turmeric, cumin, coriander and chilli powder. Stir until heated; add the beef and cook, stirring, over high heat until well coated with the spice mixture.

Add the tomatoes and 1 teaspoon salt. Simmer, covered, for 1–1$^1/_2$ hours, or until the beef is tender. Stir in the coconut milk and simmer, uncovered, for a further 5-10 minutes, or until slightly thickened.

1 kg (2 lb 4 oz) beef chuck steak

1 tablespoon ghee or oil

2 onions, chopped

2 garlic cloves, crushed

2 green chillies, chopped

1 tablespoon grated ginger

1$^1/_2$ teaspoons ground turmeric

1 teaspoon ground cumin

1 tablespoon ground coriander

$^1/_2$–1 teaspoon chilli powder

400 g (14 oz) tin tomatoes

250 ml (9 fl oz/1 cup) coconut milk

THAI BEEF AND PUMPKIN CURRY

2 tablespoons oil

750 g (1 lb 10 oz) blade (chuck) steak, thinly sliced

4 tablespoons Musaman curry paste (page 29)

2 garlic cloves, finely chopped

1 onion, sliced lengthways

6 curry leaves, torn

750 ml (26 fl oz/3 cups) coconut milk

450 g (1 lb) butternut pumpkin (squash), roughly diced

2 tablespoons chopped peanuts

1 tablespoon shaved palm sugar (jaggery), or soft brown sugar

2 tablespoons tamarind purée

2 tablespoons fish sauce

This hearty curry is delicious served with pickled vegetables (page 223) and rice.

Heat a wok or frying pan over high heat. Add the oil and swirl to coat the side. Add the meat in batches and cook for 5 minutes, or until browned. Remove the meat from the wok.

Add the curry paste, garlic, onion and curry leaves to the wok, and stir to coat. Return meat to the wok and cook, stirring, over medium heat for 2 minutes.

Add the coconut milk to the wok, then reduce the heat and simmer for 45 minutes. Add the diced pumpkin and simmer for 25–30 minutes, or until the meat and the vegetables are tender and the sauce has thickened.

Stir in the peanuts, palm sugar, tamarind purée and fish sauce, and simmer for 1 minute.

Note: The best way to cut the meat is into pieces sized approximately 5 x 5 x 2 cm (2 x 2 x $^{3}/_{4}$ inch). Then cut across the grain at a 45° angle into 5 mm ($^{1}/_{4}$ inch) thick slices.

REALLY EASY!   1½ HOURS   SERVES 6

CURRIED BEEF SAUSAGES

An old classic, this makes a cheap, cheerful and filling dinner.

Place the onion, garlic, ginger, curry powder, chilli powder, paprika and poppy seeds in a food processor and process until smooth.

Heat 1 tablespoon of the oil in a large frying pan, add the sausages in batches and cook for around 6–8 minutes, or until browned on all sides. Remove and carefully wipe out the pan with paper towels. Leave sausages to cool and slice into 1 cm ($^1/_2$ inch) thick slices.

Heat the remaining oil in pan, add the spice paste and cook, stirring, for 2 minutes, or until fragrant. Mix in tomato, mango chutney, coconut milk and sausages, and simmer, covered, for 20 minutes, stirring occasionally.

1 onion, chopped

2 garlic cloves

1 teaspoon chopped ginger

2 teaspoons curry powder

1 teaspoon chilli powder

$1^1/_2$ teaspoons paprika

3 teaspoons poppy seeds

2 tablespoons oil

1.25 kg (2 lb 12 oz) medium-size good-quality beef sausages

6 tomatoes, peeled, quartered and seeded

2 tablespoons mango chutney (page 224)

420 ml ($14^1/_2$ fl oz/ $1^2/_3$ cups) coconut milk

REALLY EASY!

1 HOUR

SERVES **6-8**

BEEF AND MUSTARD SEED CURRY

3 tablespoons oil

2 tablespoons brown mustard seeds

4 dried red chillies

1 tablespoon yellow split peas

200 g (7 oz) French shallots, thinly sliced

8 garlic cloves, crushed

1 tablespoon finely grated ginger

15 curry leaves

1/2 teaspoon ground turmeric

400 g (14 oz) tin chopped tomatoes

1 kg (2 lb 4 oz) beef chuck steak, diced

435 ml (15 1/4 fl oz/1 3/4 cups) beef stock

This comforting curry looks after itself once the initial frying of the spices is done. Stay close while cooking the spices to ensure that they do not burn. The mustard seeds, in particular, give this dish a distinctive flavour — heating them until they pop brings out their pleasant nutty taste.

Put the oil in a heavy-based saucepan over a medium heat, add the mustard seeds, chillies and split peas. As soon as the mustard seeds start to pop, add the shallots, garlic, ginger, curry leaves and turmeric. Cook for 5 minutes, then add the tomatoes, beef and stock.

Bring to the boil then reduce to a simmer, cover and cook for 2 hours, or until the beef is very tender and the sauce reduced. While cooking, skim any oil that comes to the surface and discard.

REALLY EASY!   2 1/2 HOURS   SERVES 6

Beef masala takes a while to cook but the preparation time is short. Serve with steamed coconut rice (page 40).

Heat oil in a large saucepan over high heat. Add the meat and cook in three batches for 4 minutes per batch, or until evenly browned.

Reduce the heat to medium, add the onion to the pan, cook for 5 minutes, then add garlic and cook for 1 minute. Stir in the curry paste and tamarind for 30–60 seconds, until fragrant. Return beef to the pan, add the coconut milk and the curry leaves and bring to the boil. Reduce the heat and simmer gently for 1½ hours, or until meat is tender and the sauce has reduced. Add some water if the sauce starts to stick to the base of the pan.

1 tablespoon oil

1 kg (2 lb 4 oz) chuck steak, trimmed and cut into 2 cm (³/₄ inch) cubes

1 large onion, thinly sliced

3 garlic cloves, chopped

4 tablespoons balti masala curry paste (page 25)

2 teaspoons tamarind concentrate

550 ml (19 fl oz) coconut milk

4 curry leaves

REALLY EASY! · 1³/₄ HOURS · SERVES 4

GOAN BEEF CURRY

8 cardamom pods

1 teaspoon fennel seeds

8 cloves

10 cm (4 inch) cinnamon stick

1/2 teaspoon fenugreek seeds

1/2 teaspoon ground black pepper

3 teaspoons coriander seeds

3 teaspoons cumin seeds

125 ml (4 fl oz/1/2 cup) oil

2 onions, finely chopped

6 garlic cloves, finely chopped

10 cm (4 inch) piece ginger, grated

1 kg (2 lb 4 oz) beef chuck steak, trimmed and cut into 2.5 cm (1 inch) cubes

1/2 teaspoon ground turmeric

2 teaspoons chilli powder

310 ml (10^3/4 cups/1^1/4 cups) coconut milk

This dish would traditionally be cooked in a karhai, which is a deep wok-shaped cooked dish with two handles, but if you don't have one a frying pan or casserole dish works just as well.

Remove seeds from the cardamom pods and grind them in a spice grinder or pestle and mortar with the fennel seeds, cloves, cinnamon stick, fenugreek seeds, black pepper and the coriander and cumin seeds, until they form a fine powder.

Heat oil in a karhai, heavy-based frying pan or casserole dish over medium heat and fry the onion, garlic and ginger until lightly browned. Add meat and fry until browned. Add the spices and fry for 1 minute. Add coconut milk and bring slowly to the boil. Cover, reduce heat and simmer for 1 hour, or until the meat is tender. If the liquid evaporates during cooking, add around 185 ml (6 fl oz/3/4 cup) boiling water and stir to make a thick sauce. If the sauce is still too liquid at the end of the cooking time, simmer with the lid off until it evaporates.

Note: To remove the cardamom seeds from the pods, crush the pods with the flat side of a heavy knife, then peel away the pod with your fingers, scraping out the seeds.

EASY!   1½ HOURS   SERVES 6

MADRAS BEEF CURRY

This makes quite a large portion and it's perfect for serving again the next day. It will keep in the fridge for 2–3 days.

Preheat the oven to 180°C (350°F/Gas 4). Heat the oil in a large heavy-based 3 litre (105 fl oz/12 cup) flameproof casserole dish. Cook the onion over medium heat for 4–5 minutes. Add the garlic and ginger and cook, stirring for 5 minutes, or until the onion is lightly golden, taking care not to burn it.

Add curry paste and cook, stirring, for 2 minutes, or until fragrant. Increase the heat to high, add the meat and stir constantly for 2–3 minutes, or until the meat is well coated. Add the tomato paste and stock and stir well.

Bake, covered, for 50 minutes, stirring 2–3 times during cooking, and add a little water if necessary. Reduce the oven to 160°C (315°F/Gas 2–3). Add the potato and cook for 30 minutes, then add the peas and cook for another 10 minutes, or until the potato is tender.

1 tablespoon oil

2 onions, finely chopped

3 garlic cloves, finely chopped

1 tablespoon grated ginger

4 tablespoons madras curry paste (page 28)

1 kg (2 lb 4 oz) beef chuck steak, trimmed and cut into 3 cm (1¼ inch) cubes

3 tablespoons tomato paste (concentrated purée)

250 ml (9 fl oz/1 cup) beef stock

6 new potatoes, halved

155 g (5½ oz/1 cup) frozen peas

EASY! — 2 HOURS — SERVES 6

BEEF AND LENTIL CURRY

3–4 small dried red chillies

3 tablespoons oil

2 red onions, cut into thin wedges

4 garlic cloves, finely chopped

1 tablespoon grated ginger

1 tablespoon garam masala (page 36)

3 cardamom pods, lightly crushed

1 cinnamon stick

2 teaspoons ground turmeric

750 g (1 lb 10 oz) beef chuck steak, diced

400 g (14 oz) tin chopped tomatoes

Continued →

This dish is traditionally served with rice which is cooked pilaf-style with well-browned, slow-cooked onion slices.

Soak the chillies in boiling water for 10 minutes, drain and finely chop.

Heat the oil in a large saucepan. Add the onion and cook, stirring, over medium heat for around 5 minutes, or until soft. Add the garlic and ginger, and cook for a further 2 minutes.

Add the chilli, garam masala, cardamom pods, cinnamon stick, turmeric and ¹/₂ teaspoon coarsely ground black pepper. Cook, stirring, for 2 minutes, or until fragrant. Add the beef and stir constantly for 3–4 minutes, or until the meat changes colour and is well coated in the spices.

Add the tomato, lentils, 1 teaspoon salt and 750 ml (26 fl oz/3 cups) water. Simmer, covered, for 1 hour, or until lentils are tender. Stir frequently to prevent any of the mixture sticking to the base of the pan. Add a little extra water, if necessary.

Add the pumpkin and aubergine to the pan, and cook, covered, for 20 minutes, or until the beef and vegetables are tender and the sauce thickens. Stir in spinach, tamarind purée and palm sugar, and cook, covered, for a further 10 minutes. Remove the cinnamon stick and serve.

95 g (3¹/₄ oz/¹/₂ cup) brown or green lentils

125 g (4¹/₂ oz/¹/₂ cup) red lentils

200 g (7 oz) pumpkin (squash), diced

150 g (5¹/₂ oz) baby aubergine (eggplant), quartered lengthways, diced

125 g (4¹/₂ oz) baby English spinach leaves

1 tablespoon tamarind purée

2 tablespoons shaved palm sugar (jaggery), or soft brown sugar

EASY! 2³/₄ HOURS SERVES 6

MUSAMAN CURRY WITH BEEF

2 pieces cinnamon stick

10 cardamom seeds

5 cloves

2 tablespoons oil

2 tablespoons musaman curry paste (page 29)

800 g (1 lb 12 oz) beef flank or rump steak, cut into 5 cm (2 inch) cubes

420 ml (14^{1}/$_{2}$ fl oz/ 1^{2}/$_{3}$ cups) coconut milk

250 ml (9 fl oz/1 cup) beef stock

2–3 potatoes, cut into 3 cm (1 inch) pieces

2 cm (^{3}/$_{4}$ inch) piece ginger, shredded

3 tablespoons fish sauce

3 tablespoons shaved palm sugar (jaggery), or soft brown sugar

110 g (3^{3}/$_{4}$ oz/^{2}/$_{3}$ cup) toasted salted peanuts, without skin

3 tablespoons tamarind purée

This curry has many characteristics of southern Thai cooking. Sweet flavours and spices dominate, even though the curry is moderately hot. It also has a sour taste from the tamarind and is one of the few Thai dishes with potatoes and peanuts.

Dry-fry the cinnamon stick, cardamom seeds and cloves in a saucepan or wok over a low heat. Stir all the ingredients around for 2–3 minutes or until fragrant. Remove from the pan.

Heat the oil in the same pan or wok and stir-fry the musaman paste over a medium heat for 2 minutes or until fragrant.

Add the beef to the pan and stir for 5 minutes. Add the coconut milk, stock, potatoes, ginger, fish sauce, palm sugar, three-quarters of the toasted peanuts, the tamarind purée and dry-fried spices. Reduce the heat to low and then gently simmer for 50–60 minutes until the meat is tender and the potatoes are just cooked. Taste, then adjust the seasoning if necessary. Spoon into a serving bowl and garnish with the rest of the toasted peanuts.

REALLY EASY!   1^{1}/$_{4}$ HOURS   SERVES 4

The large number of spices used in this classic dish, including a generous dose of chilli, makes it one of the most robustly flavoured curries.

Cut the steak into 2.5 cm (1 inch) cubes. Place the cumin, coriander and cardamom seeds, fenugreek, chilli powder, turmeric and mustard powder in a spice grinder and process until finely ground.

Heat the ghee in a large pan; add meat in 2 batches and cook over medium heat until browned all over. Transfer the meat to a bowl.

Add onion, ginger, garlic and cinnamon to pan, and stir over low heat until onion is soft. Add spices and meat and stir until well coated. Add vinegar, stock, sugar, and salt and pepper to taste. Cover and cook over a low heat for about $1^{1}/_{2}$ hours, or until meat is tender. Remove cinnamon stick before serving.

REALLY EASY! — 2 HOURS — SERVES 4

1 kg (2 lb 4 oz) beef chuck steak

$^{1}/_{2}$ teaspoon ground cumin

1 tablespoon coriander seeds

$^{1}/_{2}$ teaspoon cardamom seeds

1 teaspoon ground fenugreek

2 teaspoons chilli powder

1 teaspoon ground turmeric

1 teaspoon mustard powder

2 tablespoons ghee or oil

3 onions, sliced

3 teaspoons grated ginger

3 garlic cloves, crushed

1 cinnamon stick

4 tablespoons malt vinegar

125 ml (4 fl oz/$^{1}/_{2}$ cup) beef stock

1 teaspoon sugar

PENANG BEEF CURRY

2 tablespoons oil

2 tablespoons penang curry paste (page 30)

700 g (1 lb 9 oz) beef flank steak, sliced into strips

185 ml (6 fl oz/³/₄ cup) coconut milk

1 tablespoon fish sauce

1 tablespoon shaved palm sugar (jaggery), or soft brown sugar

3 tablespoons tamarind purée

This is a dry, rich, thick curry made with small amounts of coconut milk and a dry (penang) curry paste, which has red chillies, lemongrass, galangal and peanuts. It is not too hot and has a sweet and sour taste. You can use any tender cut of beef.

Heat the oil in a saucepan or wok and stir-fry the curry paste over a medium heat for 2 minutes or until fragrant.

Add the beef and stir for 5 minutes. Add nearly all of the coconut milk, the fish sauce, palm sugar and tamarind purée and reduce to a low heat. Simmer, uncovered, for 5–7 minutes. Although this is meant to be a dry curry, you can add a little more water during cooking if you feel it is drying out too much. Taste, then adjust the seasoning if necessary.

Spoon the curry into a serving bowl, then spoon the last bit of coconut milk over the top.

REALLY EASY!

25 MINUTES

SERVES 4

RED BEEF CURRY

The 'red' in this recipe refers to the red chillies in it. Take care when handling chillies and use less than the recipe states if you prefer a milder dish.

Soak chillies and kaffir lime leaves in hot water for 15 minutes. Drain chillies, split open and scrape out the seeds. Drain lime leaves.

Toast coriander seeds, caraway seeds and shrimp paste in a dry wok or non-stick pan until they are very aromatic. Grind in a food processor, spice grinder or mortar with lemongrass, onion, garlic and ginger. Add soaked chillies and lime leaves and process until it is a reasonably smooth paste.

Fry ingredients in oil for 3–4 minutes, then add coconut milk and cook gently for about 25 minutes, until the oil separates and floats to the surface.

Meanwhile, thinly slice the meat and cut into short strips no more than 2 cm (3/4 inch) wide.

Put the beef in the sauce. Add the fresh chilli and sliced beans and simmer for a few minutes until tender. Add fish sauce to taste.

6–10 dried red chillies

3 dried kaffir lime (makrut) leaves

1 tablespoon coriander seeds

1/2 teaspoon caraway seeds

1 teaspoon shrimp paste

1 lemongrass stem, white part only, chopped

1 onion, finely chopped

4 garlic cloves

2 cm (3/4 inch) piece ginger

2 tablespoons oil

800 ml (28 fl oz) coconut milk

1 kg (2 lb 4 oz) braising beef such as round or topside

1 red chilli, seeded, sliced

200 g (7 oz) green beans, sliced

2 tablespoons fish sauce

REALLY EASY! 1 HOUR + SOAKING TIME SERVES 6

SPICY BEEF CURRY WITH AUBERGINE

1 tablespoon oil

1 large onion, chopped

1–2 tablespoons green curry paste (page 27)

500 g (1 lb 2 oz) round or blade steak, cut into thick strips

185 ml (6 fl oz/³/₄ cup) coconut milk

6 kaffir lime (makrut) leaves

100 g (3 oz) pea aubergines (eggplants)

2 tablespoons fish sauce

1 teaspoon soft brown sugar

2 teaspoons finely grated lime zest

15 g (¹/₂ oz/¹/₂ cup) coriander (cilantro) leaves

30 g (1 oz/¹/₂ cup) shredded basil

Use thinly sliced slender aubergines if pea aubergines are not available.

Heat the oil in a wok or large frying pan. Add the onion and curry paste and stir for 2 minutes over medium heat until fragrant.

Heat the wok until it is very hot. Add the meat in 2 batches and stir-fry until brown. Return all the meat to the wok. Add the coconut milk, lime leaves and 3 tablespoons water. Bring to the boil, reduce heat, cover and simmer for 10 minutes. Add the aubergines and simmer, uncovered, for 10 minutes, or until both the meat and aubergines are tender.

Add the fish sauce, sugar and lime rind to the wok and mix well. Stir in the coriander and basil.

Note: Pea aubergines are tiny green aubergines sold in clusters. They are available to buy at some Asian grocers

EASY!   55 MINUTES   SERVES 4

In this festive dish of Indonesia and Malaysia, beef is cooked in a rich, thick sauce, the whole permeated with complex aromas and flavours.

Season the beef with salt and white pepper. Place the onion, ginger, garlic, turmeric, coriander and sambal oelek in a blender, and blend until smooth. Add a little water if necessary.

Heat the oil in a large saucepan, add spice paste and cook over medium heat for 5 minutes, or until fragrant. Add the beef, stir to coat in the spices and cook for 1–2 minutes. Add the coconut cream, curry leaves, lemongrass, tamarind purée, lime leaves and 500 ml (17 fl oz/2 cups) water. Reduce the heat and simmer over a low heat for 2 1/2 hours, or until the meat is tender and the sauce has thickened. Add a little water, if necessary, to prevent sauce sticking. Stir in the sugar.

1 kg (2 lb 4 oz) topside beef, cut into 1 cm (1/2 inch) thick strips

2 onions, chopped

1 tablespoon chopped ginger

3 garlic cloves, finely chopped

1 teaspoon ground turmeric

2 teaspoons ground coriander

2 1/2 tablespoons sambal oelek (page 32)

100 ml (3 1/2 fl oz) oil

400 ml (14 fl oz) coconut cream

6 curry leaves

1 lemongrass stem, bruised with the flat of a knife

100 ml (3 1/2 fl oz) tamarind purée

4 kaffir lime (makrut) leaves

1 teaspoon soft brown sugar

THAI RED BEEF CURRY WITH THAI AUBERGINES

500 g (1 lb 2 oz) round or topside steak

250 ml (9 fl oz/1 cup) coconut cream (do not shake the tin)

2 tablespoons red curry paste (page 31)

2 tablespoons fish sauce

1 tablespoon shaved palm sugar (jaggery), or soft brown sugar

5 kaffir lime (makrut) leaves, halved

500 ml (17 fl oz/2 cups) coconut milk

8 Thai apple aubergines (eggplants), halved

1 small handful Thai basil, finely shredded

There are many variations on the basic red curry, but all are distinguished by the dark shade of the sauce. Most Thai red curries are wet (not dry), and fragrant with fresh kaffir lime and Thai basil.

Cut the meat into 5 cm (2 inch) pieces, then cut across the grain at a 45° angle into 5 mm (¼ inch) thick slices.

Put the thick coconut cream from the top of the tin in a saucepan, bring to a rapid simmer over medium heat, stirring occasionally, and cook for 5–10 minutes, or until the mixture 'splits' (the oil starts to separate). Add curry paste and simmer, stirring constantly, for 5 minutes, or until fragrant.

Add meat and cook, stirring, for 3–5 minutes, or until it changes colour. Add fish sauce, palm sugar, kaffir lime leaves, coconut milk and remaining coconut cream, and simmer for 1 hour, or until the meat is tender and the sauce slightly thickened.

Add the aubergine and cook for 10 minutes, or until tender. If the sauce is too thick, add a little water. Stir in the basil leaves and serve.

EASY! · 1¾ HOURS · SERVES 4

LAMB MADRAS

In India, sheep or goat meat is often used in this curry. As goat can be tough, we have used lamb.

Rub the cubed lamb with ground turmeric. In a small frying pan dry-fry coriander seeds over low heat until aromatic. Remove and repeat with cumin seeds and chillies. Grind all to a powder in a mortar and pestle or spice grinder. Add six curry leaves, garlic and ginger and grind to a paste.

Dry-fry fennel seeds in pan until brown Dissolve tamarind in 125 ml (4 fl oz/^{1}/$_2$ cup) hot water. Heat oil or ghee in a casserole dish over low heat and fry onions for 5–10 minutes until soft. Add chilli paste; cook for a few minutes or until aromatic. Add meat; toss well to mix with paste. Add 500 ml (17 fl oz/ 2 cups) of coconut milk and 3 tablespoons water. Bring to boil, then simmer over medium heat for 10 minutes, or until the liquid reduces.

Add remaining coconut milk, cinnamon stick, cardamom pods, fennel seeds and salt and pepper. Cover partially. Cook over medium heat, for 1 hour until meat is tender, stirring occasionally. Add the tamarind. Stir until oil separates out from meat, then remove oil with a spoon. Remove pan from the heat. Stir well and add remaining curry leaves.

900 g (2 lb) boneless leg or shoulder of lamb, cut into 2.5 cm (1 inch) cubes

1 ^{1}/$_2$ teaspoons ground turmeric

2 tablespoons coriander seeds

2 teaspoons cumin seeds

10 dried chillies

12 curry leaves

10 garlic cloves, roughly chopped

5 cm (2 inch) piece ginger, roughly chopped

1 teaspoon fennel seeds

1 tablespoon tamarind paste

4 tablespoons oil or ghee

3 large onions, sliced

625 ml (21 ^{1}/$_2$ fl oz/ 2 ^{1}/$_2$ cups) coconut milk

7.5 cm (3 inch) piece cinnamon stick

6 cardamom pods

EASY! | 2^3/$_4$ HOURS | SERVES 4

MUGHUL-STYLE LAMB

6 garlic cloves, roughly chopped

5 cm (2 inch) piece ginger, roughly chopped

3 tablespoons blanched almonds

2 onions, thinly sliced

680 g (1 1/2 lb) boneless leg or shoulder of lamb, cut into 3 cm (1 inch) cubes

2 teaspoons coriander seeds

2 tablespoons ghee

7 cardamom pods

5 whole cloves

1 cinnamon stick

310 ml (10 3/4 fl oz/1 1/4 cups) cream

1/2 teaspoon cayenne pepper

1/2 teaspoon garam masala (page 36)

Blend garlic, ginger, almonds and 1/3 cup of onions in a blender or food processor. Or, finely chop them with a knife, or grind in a pestle and mortar. Add a little water to make a smooth paste. Put in a bowl with the lamb and mix well to coat meat. Cover. Marinate in the fridge for 2 hours, or overnight.

Place a small frying pan over low heat, dry-fry the coriander seeds until aromatic, then grind to a fine powder using a spice grinder or pestle and mortar.

Heat ghee in a karhai or casserole dish. Add cloves, cardamom pods and cinnamon stick and, after a few seconds, add the remaining onions and fry until soft and golden brown. Transfer onions to a plate.

Fry meat and marinade in pan until mixture is dry and starting to brown. Add 125 ml (4 fl oz/1/2 cup) hot water to pan, cover tightly and cook over low heat for 30 minutes, stirring occasionally.

Add ground coriander, cream, cayenne pepper, cooked onions and 1 teaspoon salt to pan, cover and simmer for 30 minutes, or until lamb is tender. Stir occasionally. Remove cardamom pods, cloves and cinnamon stick, then stir in the garam masala.

EASY!

1 1/4 HOURS + MARINATING TIME

SERVES 4

LAMB RIZALA

This recipe is a study in how to produce melt-in-the-mouth tender, flavoursome meat. Traditionally, rizala featured mutton, so slow, gentle cooking was the ideal method, but this applies equally to lamb shoulder. The yoghurt further tenderizes the meat, helping it absorb the aromatics.

Put 3 tablespoons of water in a food processor or in a large mortar with a pestle, along with the onions, ginger, garlic and cinnamon, and process or pound to a smooth paste.

Heat ghee or oil in a heavy-based saucepan over high heat. Brown lamb in batches and set aside.

Reduce the heat to low, add the onion paste and cook for 5 minutes, stirring constantly. Put the lamb back into the pan, and stir to combine, add the yoghurt a spoon at a time, stirring well to incorporate. Add the chicken stock and crisp fried onion. Bring to a simmer, cover and cook over low heat for 2 hours. While cooking, skim any oil that comes to the surface and discard.

When lamb is tender, add chillies, sugar and lime juice, and cook for 5 minutes more before serving.

2 onions, chopped

1 tablespoon grated ginger

4 garlic cloves, crushed

1 teaspoon ground cinnamon

3 tablespoons ghee or oil

1 kg (2 lb 4 oz) lamb shoulder, diced

125 g (4^1/$_2$ oz/^{1}/$_2$ cup) plain yoghurt

250 ml (9 fl oz/1 cup) chicken stock

40 g (1^1/$_2$ oz/^{1}/$_2$ cup) crisp fried onion

3 red chillies seeded, thinly sliced

1 tablespoon sugar

3 tablespoons lime juice

REALLY EASY!   2^1/$_2$ HOURS   SERVES 6

SOUR LAMB AND BAMBOO CURRY

CURRY PASTE

1 teaspoon white peppercorns

1 teaspoon shrimp paste, wrapped in foil

30 g (1 oz) dried shrimp

6 spring onions (scallions), sliced

60 g (2¼ oz) jalapeño chillies (in brine), sliced

2 lemongrass stems, white part only, thinly sliced

6 garlic cloves, crushed

4 coriander (cilantro) roots, chopped

2 teaspoons ground ginger

1 teaspoon chilli powder

4 tablespoons fish sauce

4 tablespoons lime juice

1 teaspoon ground turmeric

500 g (1 lb 2 oz boneless lamb leg, trimmed of excess fat

1 tablespoon oil

Continued →

Bamboo shoots are used mainly in Southeast Asian cooking. When fresh, they have a lovely crisp, nutty bitterness to them. They are available in Asian food stores, but the tinned variety makes an acceptable substitute. Along with the green beans and lamb, they provide texture to this curry.

Dry-fry the peppercorns and the shrimp paste in a frying pan over medium–high heat for 2–3 minutes, or until fragrant. Allow to cool and remove the foil. Using a mortar with a pestle, or a spice grinder, crush or grind to a powder. Process the dried shrimp in a food processor until it becomes very finely shredded — forming a 'floss'.

Put the crushed peppercorns, shrimp paste and dried shrimp with the remaining curry paste ingredients in a food processor, or in a mortar with a pestle, and process or pound to a smooth paste.

Slice lamb into strips 5 x 2 cm (2 x $^3/_4$ inch) and 3 mm ($^1/_8$ inch) thick. Heat oil in a heavy-based casserole dish over a medium heat. Add about 3 tablespoons of paste. Stir constantly, adding the palm sugar. When the palm sugar has dissolved add the lamb, stirring for about 7 minutes, or until lightly golden.

Add the coconut cream, 250 ml (9 fl oz/1 cup) water, tamarind, fish sauce and bamboo. Bring to the boil then reduce heat and simmer for about 20 minutes, or until tender. Add the beans and simmer for a further 3 minutes.

1 tablespoon shaved palm sugar (jaggery), or soft brown sugar

250 ml (9 fl oz/1 cup) coconut cream

3 tablespoons tamarind purée

1$^1/_2$ tablespoons fish sauce

400 g (14 oz) tinned bamboo pieces, drained and cut into thick wedges

200 g (7 oz) green beans, cut into 4 cm (1$^1/_2$ inch) lengths

EASY!

50 MINUTES

SERVES 2

BALTI-STYLE LAMB

1 kg (2 lb 4 oz) lamb leg steaks, cut into 3 cm (1 inch) cubes

5 tablespoons balti masala paste (page 25)

2 tablespoons ghee or oil

3 garlic cloves, crushed

1 tablespoon garam masala (page 36)

1 large onion, finely chopped

2 tablespoons chopped coriander (cilantro) leaves, plus extra for garnish

Baltistan may lie high in the mountains of north Pakistan, but Birmingham, England, has become the international launch pad of Balti cuisine. Distinctive for its use of the two-handled karhai pot, it also features its own masala paste, which is herby and fragrant with cardamom.

Preheat the oven to 190°C (375°F/Gas 5). Put the meat, 1 tablespoon of balti masala paste and 375 ml (13 fl oz/1^1/$_2$ cups) boiling water in a large casserole dish or karahi, and combine. Cook, covered, in oven for 30–40 minutes, or until almost cooked through. Drain, reserving the stock.

Heat ghee or oil in a wok, add garlic and garam masala, and stir-fry over medium heat for 1 minute. Add onion and cook for 5–7 minutes, until the onion is golden brown. Increase the heat, add remaining balti masala paste and lamb. Cook for 5 minutes to brown meat. Slowly add the stock and simmer over low heat, stirring occasionally, for 15 minutes.

Add 185 ml (6 fl oz/^{3}/$_4$ cup) of water and chopped coriander leaves and simmer for 15 minutes, or until meat is tender and the sauce has thickened slightly. Season with salt and pepper and garnish with coriander leaves.

EASY!

1^3/$_4$ HOURS

SERVES 4

BASIC LAMB CURRY

Ask the butcher to bone a 2.2 kg (5 lb) leg of lamb. This will yield about 1.5 kg (3 lb 5 oz) meat.

Heat 1 tablespoon of the oil in a large saucepan, add a third of the lamb and cook over high heat for 4 minutes, or until browned. Remove. Repeat twice more with the remaining lamb and 2 more tablespoons oil. Remove all the lamb from the pan.

Heat the remaining oil in the saucepan. Add onion and cook over medium heat, stirring frequently, for 10 minutes, or until golden. Add garlic, ginger and chilli, and cook for 2 minutes, then add the ground spices and cook, stirring, for a further 3 minutes, or until fragrant.

Add tomato, tomato paste, the lamb and 1 teaspoon salt. Mix thoroughly, then reduce heat and simmer, covered, for $1^{1}/_{2}$ hours, or until the meat is tender. Stir occasionally.

Uncover, increase heat and cook for 10 minutes to allow the sauce to reduce and thicken. Garnish with coriander and serve with rice or boiled potatoes.

1.5 kg (3 lb 5 oz) lamb, cut into 3 cm (1 inch) cubes

4 tablespoons oil

2 large onions, finely chopped

4–6 garlic cloves, chopped

1 tablespoon grated ginger

2 small red chillies, seeded, chopped

1 tablespoon ground cumin

1 tablespoon ground coriander

2 teaspoons ground turmeric

$^{1}/_{2}$ teaspoon chilli powder

2 x 400 g (14 oz) tins crushed tomatoes

1 tablespoon tomato paste (concentrated purée)

4 tablespoons chopped coriander (cilantro)

EASY! | **3** HOURS | SERVES **6**

4 garlic cloves, crushed

1$\frac{1}{2}$ tablespoons chopped ginger

2$\frac{1}{2}$ tablespoons lemon juice

1 kg (2 lb 4 oz) lamb leg or shoulder, diced

1$\frac{1}{2}$ tablespoons coriander seeds

$\frac{1}{4}$ teaspoon black peppercorns

2 tomatoes, chopped

2 teaspoons tomato paste (concentrated purée)

3 long green chillies, seeded, chopped

1 handful coriander (cilantro) stems and roots, roughly chopped

3 tablespoons oil

250 ml (9 fl oz/1 cup) chicken stock

2 tablespoons plain yoghurt

The Swahili cuisine of the Kenyan coast is a vibrant one with colourful and richly spiced dishes.

Put garlic, ginger, lemon juice and enough water to form a paste in a food processor, or in a mortar and pestle. Process or pound to a smooth paste. Put lamb into a non-metallic bowl, add garlic paste and combine well. Cover and refrigerate for 2 hours.

Dry-fry coriander seeds and peppercorns in a frying pan over medium–high heat for 2–3 minutes Allow to cool. Using a mortar and pestle, or a spice grinder, grind to a powder.

Put ground spices, tomato, tomato paste, chillies and coriander stems and roots in a food processor, or a mortar and pestle, and create a smooth paste.

Heat oil in a heavy-based saucepan over medium–high heat. Brown lamb in batches. When lamb is done, return to pan with tomato chilli paste and stock. Bring to the boil then reduce to a simmer, cover and cook for 1$\frac{1}{2}$ hours, remove lid and then cook for 15 minutes, or until lamb is tender. While cooking, skim any oil on the surface and discard. Remove from heat and stir through yoghurt.

EASY!   2$\frac{1}{2}$ HOURS + 2HRS MARINATING TIME   SERVES 6

LAMB KORMA

This mild dish needs to be cooked very slowly to allow the subtle flavours emerge.

Put meat in a bowl, add yoghurt. Mix to coat well.

Place a small frying pan over low heat and dry-fry coriander seeds until aromatic. Remove and dry-fry cumin seeds. Grind roasted mixture to a fine powder using a spice grinder or pestle and mortar. Remove seeds from cardamom pods and grind.

Roughly chop one onion and thinly slice the other. Put the roughly chopped onion with the ground spices, coconut, poppy seeds, chillies, garlic, ginger, cashew nuts, cloves and cinnamon in a blender, add 125 ml (4 fl oz/$^1/_2$ cup) water and then process to a smooth paste. Instead of a blender, you can use a pestle and mortar, then add water.

Heat oil in a casserole dish over medium heat. Add sliced onion; fry until lightly browned. Pour blended mixture into pan, add salt. Cook over low heat for 1 minute, or until sauce thickens. Add lamb with yoghurt; slowly bring to a boil. Cover tightly. Simmer for 1$^1/_2$ hours, or until meat is very tender. Stir occasionally. If needed, add a little more water to make a thick sauce.

900 g (2 lb) boneless leg or shoulder of lamb, cut into 3 cm (1$^1/_4$ inch) cubes

2 tablespoons plain yoghurt

1 tablespoon coriander seeds

2 teaspoons cumin seeds

5 cardamom pods

2 onions

2 tablespoons grated coconut

1 tablespoon white poppy seeds

3 green chillies, roughly chopped

4 garlic cloves, crushed

5 cm (2 inch) piece ginger, grated

1 tablespoon cashew nuts

6 cloves

$^1/_4$ teaspoon ground cinnamon

2 tablespoons oil

EASY! 1$^3/_4$ HOURS SERVES 4

ROGAN JOSH

1 kg (2 lb 4 oz) boned leg of lamb

1 tablespoon ghee or oil

2 onions, chopped

125 g (4$^1/_4$ oz/$^1/_2$ cup) plain yoghurt

1 teaspoon chilli powder

1 tablespoon ground coriander

2 teaspoons ground cumin

1 teaspoon ground cardamom

$^1/_2$ teaspoon ground cloves

1 teaspoon ground turmeric

3 garlic cloves, crushed

1 tablespoon grated ginger

400 g (14 oz) tin chopped tomatoes

3 tablespoons slivered almonds

1 teaspoon garam masala (page 36)

Ghee is a clarified butter — that is, butter that has been melted and boiled to remove milk solids and water. It has a strong nutty flavour and a rich, toasted aroma, which is used to advantage in meat and vegetable curries, lentil dals and rice dishes. You can buy it from Asian and Indian food stores.

Trim the lamb of any excess fat and sinew, and cut it into 2.5 cm (1 inch) cubes.

Heat ghee in a large saucepan, add onion and cook, stirring, for 5 minutes, or until soft. Stir in yoghurt, chilli powder, coriander, cumin, cardamom, cloves, turmeric, garlic and ginger. Add 1 teaspoon of salt and the tomato and simmer for 5 minutes.

Add lamb and stir until coated. Cover and cook over low heat, stirring occasionally, for 1–1$^1/_2$ hours, or until lamb is tender. Remove lid and simmer until liquid thickens.

Meanwhile, toast almonds in a dry frying pan over medium heat for 3–4 minutes, until golden brown. Remove from the pan at once to prevent burning.

Add garam masala to curry and mix through well. Sprinkle slivered almonds over the top and serve.

EASY! | 2 HOURS | SERVES 6-8

This is a South Asian curry dish and its name, 'dopiaza', literally means 'having two onions'.

Slice half the onions and set aside; roughly chop the remaining onions.

Place chopped onion, garlic, ginger, chilli, paprika, fresh and ground coriander, cumin seeds and yoghurt in a food processor and process until a smooth paste is formed.

Heat the ghee in a large pan; add the sliced onion and cook over medium heat for 10 minutes or until golden brown. Remove the onion from the pan using a slotted spoon and drain on paper towels.

Put lamb into the pan in batches and cook over high heat until browned. Remove from pan and cover loosely with foil.

Add onion paste to the pan; cook for 5 minutes, or until ghee starts to separate from onion. Reduce heat to low, return meat to pan with the cardamom, cover and cook for 1 hour or until meat is tender.

Add fried onion and sprinkle garam masala over lamb; cover and continue cooking for 15 minutes.

1 kg (2 lb 4 oz) onions

5 garlic cloves

5 cm (2 inch) piece ginger, grated

2 red chillies

1 teaspoon paprika

4 tablespoons chopped coriander (cilantro) leaves

2 tablespoons ground coriander

2 teaspoons black cumin seeds

4 tablespoons yoghurt

4 tablespoons ghee or oil

1 kg (2 lb 4 oz) diced lamb

6 cardamom pods, lightly crushed

1 teaspoon garam masala (page 36)

EASY! · 2½ HOURS · SERVES 4-6

LAMB KOFTA

LAMB KOFTA

1 kg (2 lb 4 oz) minced (ground) lamb

1 onion, finely chopped

2 small green chillies, finely chopped

3 teaspoons grated ginger

3 garlic cloves, crushed

4 tablespoons fresh breadcrumbs

1 egg, lightly beaten

1 teaspoon ground cardamom

2 tablespoons ghee or oil

Continued →

Every nation seems to have a version of kofta, ranging from meatballs and croquettes to rissoles and dumplings. This is a delicious Indian version.

Line a baking tray with baking paper or plastic wrap. Place lamb in a large bowl with onion, chilli, ginger, garlic, breadcrumbs, egg and cardamom. Season and mix together. Roll level tablespoons of the mixture into balls, and place on the tray.

Heat ghee in a large frying pan, add the meatballs in batches and cook for 10 minutes, or until they are browned all over. Remove from the pan.

Make the sauce by heating the ghee in the same pan. Add onion, chilli, ginger, garlic and turmeric, and cook, stirring, over a low heat for 8 minutes, or until the onion is soft. Add coriander, cumin, chilli powder, vinegar, meatballs and 330 ml (11¼ fl oz/ 1⅓ cups) water, and stir gently. Simmer, covered, for 30 minutes.

Stir in the combined yoghurt and coconut milk, and simmer, partially covered, for another 10 minutes. Serve with rice.

SAUCE

1 tablespoon ghee or oil

1 onion, sliced

1 green chilli, finely chopped

3 teaspoons grated ginger

2 garlic cloves, crushed

1 teaspoon ground turmeric

3 teaspoons ground coriander

2 teaspoons ground cumin

1 teaspoon chilli powder

2 tablespoons white vinegar

185 g (6½ oz/¾ cup) plain yoghurt

310 ml (10¾ fl oz/ 1¼ cups) coconut milk

MINCED LAMB WITH ORANGE

3 tablespoons oil

2 onions, finely diced

4 garlic cloves, crushed

3 teaspoons finely grated ginger

2 teaspoons ground cumin

2 teaspoons ground coriander

$1/2$ teaspoon ground turmeric

$1/2$ teaspoon cayenne pepper

1 teaspoon garam masala (page 36)

1 kg (2 lb 4 oz) minced (ground) lamb

4 tablespoons plain yoghurt

250 ml (9 fl oz/1 cup) orange juice

2 teaspoons orange zest

1 bay leaf

1 long green chilli, seeded, thinly sliced

1 handful each coriander (cilantro) leaves and mint, roughly chopped

There is probably no meat more versatile than lamb. This non-traditional curry blends aromatic ground spices with the sweetness of orange juice and the cleansing freshness of green chillies and mint. It is a thick, wet curry, ideal for serving with bread for mopping up any leftovers.

Heat the oil in a large heavy-based frying pan over a medium heat. Add the onion, garlic and ginger and sauté for 5 minutes. Add cumin, coriander, turmeric, cayenne pepper and garam masala, and cook for a further 5 minutes.

Increase heat to high, add lamb, and cook, stirring constantly to break the meat up. Add the yoghurt, a tablespoon at a time, stirring so it combines well. Add the orange juice, zest and bay leaf.

Bring to the boil then reduce to a simmer, cover and cook for 45 minutes, or until tender. While cooking, skim any oil that comes to the surface and discard. Season well to taste then stir through the green chilli, coriander and mint before serving.

EASY! 1 1/4 HOURS SERVES 6

This curry is known as a 'gulai', which is the richest of the Indonesian curries.

Combine the lamb, onion, oil and $1/4$ teaspoon each of salt and pepper.

Heat a wok or heavy-based pan until very hot; add the lamb and onion mixture in several batches and brown very well. Using tongs or a slotted spoon, remove all the meat from the wok, leaving any oil.

Combine the lemongrass, garlic, galangal, ginger, turmeric, chilli and shrimp paste in a food processor and process, adding the extra oil, until a smooth paste is formed.

Reheat the wok; add the spice paste and cook it over medium heat for 3 minutes, stirring constantly (take care the paste does not burn). Add the lamb and onion mixture, cinnamon, cloves and coconut milk.

Simmer, uncovered, for $1^1/2$ hours, stirring every now and then, until the lamb is very tender.

750 g (1 lb 10 oz) diced lamb

2 large onions, chopped

3 tablespoons oil

2 lemongrass stems, white part only, sliced

6 garlic cloves

2.5 cm (1 inch) piece galangal, roughly chopped

10 cm (4 inch) piece ginger, roughly chopped

$2^1/2$ teaspoons ground turmeric

2 red chillies, roughly chopped

1 teaspoon shrimp paste

2 tablespoons oil, extra

2 cinnamon sticks

pinch ground cloves

750 ml (26 fl oz/3 cups) coconut milk

EASY! 2¼ HOURS SERVES 4-6

LAMB SHANK AND YOGHURT CURRY

3 tablespoons coriander seeds

2 teaspoons cumin seeds

1 teaspoon cloves

1 teaspoon black peppercorns

$^1/_2$ teaspoon cayenne pepper

1 teaspoon ground turmeric

2 tablespoons chopped ginger

6 garlic cloves, chopped

1 small onion, chopped

2 tablespoons ghee or oil

Continued →

This is not a curry to make at the last minute, but the slow cooking produces wonderfully tender meat, while also allowing for the subtle aromas and flavours of the spices to emerge and blend. Lamb shank is ideal for this and the use of yoghurt thickens the sauce and rounds off the dish.

Preheat oven to 160°C (315°F/Gas 2–3). In a frying pan over medium–high heat, dry-fry the coriander seeds, cumin seeds, cloves, peppercorns, cayenne pepper and turmeric for 2–3 minutes, or until fragrant. Allow to cool. Using a mortar and pestle, or a spice grinder, crush to a powder.

Put the ground spices with the ginger, garlic, onion and 3 tablespoons water in a food processor, or in a mortar with a pestle, and process or pound to a smooth paste.

Heat ghee or oil over medium–high heat in a large heavy-based frying pan. Brown the shanks in batches and set aside. Reduce the heat to low. Add the ginger spice paste to frying pan, and cook for 5–8 minutes. Add the cinnamon, bay leaves and yoghurt to the pan, a spoonful at a time, stirring well so it incorporates smoothly. Add chicken stock and stir well to combine.

Put the shanks into a large heavy-based ovenproof dish that will fit them in a single layer, then pour the yoghurt sauce over the top of the shanks. Turn the shanks so they are coated with the sauce, and cover with a lid, or foil. Bake in the oven for about 3 hours, or until the lamb is falling from the bone, turning the shanks halfway through cooking. When you remove from the oven, skim any oil that comes to the surface and discard.

Remove the shanks from the sauce onto a serving platter. Season the sauce well to taste, stirring to mix before spooning over the shanks.

6 lamb shanks

3 cinnamon sticks

2 bay leaves

375 g (13 oz/1$\frac{1}{2}$ cups) plain yoghurt

625 ml (21$\frac{1}{2}$ fl oz/ 2$\frac{1}{2}$ cups) chicken stock

EASY!   **4** HOURS   SERVES **6**

2¹/₂ teaspoons cumin seeds

1 teaspoon ground turmeric

125 g (4¹/₂ oz/¹/₂ cup) plain yoghurt

2 teaspoons clear vinegar

1 tablespoon ginger juice (see Note, page 227)

3 teaspoons chilli powder

1 kg (2 lb 4 oz) lamb leg, cut into 2.5 cm (1 inch) cubes

2 potatoes, cut into 2.5 cm (1 inch) cubes

oil, for deep-frying

4 garlic cloves, crushed

¹/₂ teaspoon sugar

4 onions, sliced

2.5 cm (1 inch) piece cinnamon stick

2 cardamom pods, crushed

2 Indian bay leaves (cassia leaves)

1 tablespoon tomato paste (concentrated purée)

Place a small frying pan over a low heat and dry-fry 2 teaspoons of cumin seeds until aromatic. Grind seeds to a fine powder using a spice grinder or a pestle and mortar. Combine 1 teaspoon salt and ¹/₂ teaspoon turmeric with cumin, yoghurt, vinegar, ginger juice and chilli powder in a bowl. Add the lamb and coat well. Cover and marinate for 2 hours in the fridge.

Coat the potatoes with the remaining ¹/₂ teaspoon of turmeric. Fill a casserole dish one-third full with oil and heat to 180°C (350°F), or until a cube of bread dropped in the oil browns in 15 seconds. Fry potato until golden, remove and drain on paper towels. Let oil cool a little, then pour out all but 2 tablespoons. Place pan over medium heat and fry the remaining cumin seeds until they pop. Add the garlic, sugar, onions, cinnamon stick and cardamom pods, and fry until golden.

Add meat and fry until browned (use extra oil if needed). Add bay leaves, tomato paste and 250 ml (9 fl oz/1 cup) water and reduce heat. Cover and simmer 1 hour, or until lamb is tender. If sauce is a little thin, simmer with lid off until it thickens. Toss potatoes through meat before serving.

EASY! · 1¹/₂ HOURS +MARINATING TIME · SERVES 6

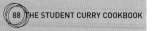

MINTED LAMB CURRY

Wonderfully fresh tasting, mint is more often associated with chutneys, salads and teas than curries, but this simple dish proves that it can work well in this arena, too. Here, it is combined with coriander, green chillies and lemon juice, creating a refreshing curry.

Place the lamb, onion, garlic, ginger, cayenne, turmeric, and chicken stock in a heavy-based saucepan over medium heat. Bring to a simmer, reduce to low heat, cover and cook for 2 hours. Skim the surface to remove any oil and discard.

Put the coriander leaves and stems, mint leaves, green chillies, lemon juice and 2 tablespoons of cooking liquid from the curry in a food processor, or in a mortar with a pestle, and process or pound to a smooth consistency. Pour into lamb mixture, then put back on the heat until it just comes back up to a simmer. Add the sugar, season well to taste and serve.

1 kg (2 lb 4 oz) lamb shoulder, cut into 2 cm ($^3/_4$ inch) dice

4 onions, thinly sliced

3 garlic cloves, crushed

3 teaspoons finely chopped ginger

$^1/_2$ teaspoon cayenne pepper

1 teaspoon ground turmeric

125 ml (4 fl oz/$^1/_2$ cup) chicken stock

1 handful coriander (cilantro) leaves and stems

1 handful mint

3 long green chillies

3 tablespoons lemon juice

1 teaspoon sugar

REALLY EASY!   2$^1/_4$ HOURS   SERVES 6

PORK

Pork is popular in curries as it can be teamed with rich flavours. Many cuts of pork can be used in curries, though the leaner cuts, such as fillet, tend to be cooked for less time than pork belly, pork shoulder or pork neck, which have long cooking times.

1.5 kg (3 lb 5 oz) pork (shoulder or forequarter)

6 teaspoons crushed garlic

1 tablespoon finely grated ginger

1 tablespoon ground cumin

1 teaspoon ground black pepper

1 1/2 teaspoons ground cinnamon

1 teaspoon ground nutmeg

3/4 teaspoon ground cloves

250 ml (9 fl oz/1 cup) white vinegar

3 tablespoons ghee or oil

3 onions, finely chopped

125 ml (4 fl oz/1/2 cup) tomato juice

3 red chillies, seeded, chopped

1 tablespoon soft brown sugar

The flavour of this curry gets better with time. Cook it up to 3 days ahead, then refrigerate or, freeze for up to 1 month.

Remove the skin from pork and then cut the meat into 3 cm (1 1/4 inch) cubes. Put in a large glass or ceramic bowl.

Combine garlic, ginger, cumin, pepper, cinnamon, nutmeg, cloves and half the vinegar, add to bowl. Turn the meat to coat it with marinade, cover and refrigerate overnight. Drain the pork and reserve the marinade.

Heat the ghee or oil in a large pan and cook the onion until it is reduced and slightly golden. Add the pork, cook over a high heat until it changes colour.

Add the tomato juice, the remaining vinegar, chilli and 1 teaspoon salt. Simmer on low heat, covered, for 1 1/2 hours or until the liquid has reduced and thickened and the meat is tender. Stir in sugar.

REALLY EASY! · 2 1/2 HOURS + MARINATING TIME · SERVES 6

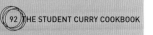

BURMESE PORK CURRY

Pork is a favourite meat across much of India and Southeast Asia and it is often teamed with other rich flavours.

Place lemongrass, onion, garlic, ginger, chillies, fenugreek seeds, yellow mustard seeds, paprika and Worchestershire sauce in a food processor or blender, and process to a thick paste.

Place pork in a bowl, sprinkle with fish sauce and 1/4 teaspoon ground black pepper, and toss to coat. Place the potato and the onion in another bowl, add 3–4 tablespoons of the paste and toss to coat. Add remaining paste to the pork mixture and mix well.

Heat 1 tablespoon of oil in a saucepan or wok over medium heat. Add pork mixture and cook in batches, stirring, for 8 minutes, or until meat begins to brown. Add oil as necessary. Remove from pan. Add potato and onion, and cook, stirring, for 5 minutes, or until soft and starting to brown.

Return meat to the pan and add 750 ml (26 fl oz/ 3 cups) water, 250 ml (9 fl oz/1 cup) at a time, stirring with each addition. Stir in mango chutney, reduce the heat and simmer for 30 minutes, or until meat and potatoes are tender.

EASY! 1½ HOURS SERVES 6

2 lemongrass stems, white part only, sliced

1 red onion, chopped

1 garlic clove

1 teaspoon grated ginger

2 large dried red chillies

1 teaspoon fenugreek seeds, dry-roasted and ground

1 teaspoon yellow mustard seeds, dry-roasted and ground

2 teaspoons paprika

2 tablespoons Worcestershire sauce

750 g (1 lb 10 oz) lean boneless shoulder pork, cut into 2.5 cm (1 inch) cubes

2 tablespoons fish sauce

6 new potatoes, peeled and sliced

2 small red onions, diced

2 tablespoons oil

2 tablespoons mango chutney

RED PORK CURRY

4 dried red chillies

125 ml (4 fl oz/$^1/_2$ cup) boiling water

1 onion, chopped

2 garlic cloves, chopped

2 cm ($^3/_4$ inch) piece ginger, grated

1 tablespoon finely chopped lemongrass, white part only

500 g (1 lb 2 oz) pork fillet, sliced into medallions

2 tablespoons tamarind concentrate

2 tablespoons ghee or oil

$^1/_2$ cup (125 ml/4 fl oz) coconut milk

Tamarind has a fruity, sour flavour and is widely used in Asian cooking. It's not usually available fresh, but is commonly found in jars as tamarind purée. If unavailable, you can soak tamarind pulp in hot water, then strain it and use the liquid.

Put the chillies in a heatproof bowl, pour over the boiling water and soak for 10 minutes.

Place the chillies and soaking water, onion, garlic, ginger and lemongrass in a food processor and process until a paste is formed.

Place the pork in a shallow dish, add the chilli paste and tamarind, and mix to combine. Cover and refrigerate for 1 hour.

Heat the ghee in a wok; add the pork in batches, and cook over high heat for 5 minutes or until the pork browns. Return all the meat to the pan with any leftover marinade, stir in the coconut milk, and simmer for 5 minutes or until heated through.

REALLY EASY!   40 MINUTES + MARINATING TIME   SERVES 4

This is quite a fiery Indian curry. It's great served with with boiled rice and poppadoms.

Trim the pork of any excess fat and sinew and cut into bite-size pieces.

Heat oil in a saucepan, add meat in small batches and cook over medium heat for 5–7 minutes, or until browned. Remove from the pan.

Add the onion, garlic, ginger, garam masala and mustard seeds to the pan, and cook, stirring, for 5 minutes, or until the onion is soft.

Return all the meat to the pan, add the vindaloo paste and then cook, stirring, for 2 minutes. Add 625 ml (21$\frac{1}{2}$ fl oz/2$\frac{1}{2}$ cups) water and bring to the boil. Reduce the heat and then simmer, covered, for 1$\frac{1}{2}$ hours, or until the meat is tender.

1 kg (2 lb 4 oz) pork fillets

3 tablespoons oil

2 onions, finely chopped

4 garlic cloves, finely chopped

1 tablespoon finely chopped ginger

1 tablespoon garam masala (page 36)

2 teaspoons brown mustard seeds

4 tablespoons vindaloo paste (page 33)

THAI SWEET PORK AND PINEAPPLE CURRY

500 g (1 lb 2 oz) boneless pork leg, trimmed

1 tablespoon oil

3 garlic cloves, crushed

125 ml (4 fl oz/$^1/_2$ cup) malt vinegar

3 tablespoons shaved palm sugar (jaggery)

3 tablespoons tomato paste (concentrated purée)

1 tomato, cut into wedges

1 onion, cut into thin wedges

90 g (3$^1/_4$ oz/$^1/_2$ cup) chopped pineapple

$^1/_2$ telegraph (long) cucumber, halved lengthways, seeded, sliced

$^1/_2$ red capsicum (pepper), cut into strips

2$^1/_2$ tablespoons jalapeño chillies (in brine), chopped

2 spring onions (scallions), cut into 5 cm (2 inch) pieces

1 small handful coriander (cilantro) leaves

This curry is a vibrant mix of fresh ingredients, including pineapple, tomatoes, cucumber and coriander — as well as sweet and sour seasonings such as vinegar and palm sugar. This combination makes it a great summer dish: it has a refreshing, slightly spicy and sweet flavour.

Cut the pork into 3 cm (1$^1/_4$ inch) cubes. Heat the oil in a large saucepan over medium heat. Add the pork and garlic and cook for 4–5 minutes, or until pork is lightly browned.

In another saucepan, stir the vinegar, palm sugar, $^1/_2$ teaspoon salt and the tomato paste over medium heat for 3 minutes, or until palm sugar is dissolved.

Add the vinegar mixture to the pork along with the tomato, onion, pineapple, cucumber, capsicum, and jalapeños. Bring to the boil then reduce to a simmer and cook for 8–10 minutes, or until the pork is tender. Stir in the spring onions and coriander and serve.

REALLY EASY! · 45 MINUTES · SERVES 4

FRIED PORK CURRY

This is a great curry to cook when there's not much in the cupboard as it needs relatively few ingredients. Serve with rice.

Place onion, garlic and ginger in a food processor and process until a thick, rough paste is formed.

Heat the peanut oil and sesame oil in a large pan; add the paste and cook it over medium heat for about 15 minutes until it becomes a golden brown colour and has oil around the edges. Add the chilli powder, turmeric and pork, and stir well for a few minutes until pork is well coated with the mixture.

Add the vinegar and water, cover and simmer gently for 1¹/₂ hours or until the meat is tender. If necessary reduce the liquid by removing the lid and allowing the sauce to evaporate. Season with salt to taste (the dish will need more if you use water instead of stock) and sprinkle on coriander.

310 g (10¹/₂ oz/2 cups) roughly chopped onion

15 garlic cloves, crushed

4 tablespoons finely chopped ginger

3 tablespoons peanut oil

1 tablespoon sesame oil

1¹/₂ teaspoons chilli powder

1 teaspoon ground turmeric

1.5 kg (3 lb 5 oz) boneless pork, cut into 3 cm (1¹/₄ inch) cubes

1 tablespoon whote vinegar

250 ml (9 fl oz/1 cup) water or stock

2 tablespoons coriander (cilantro) leaves

REALLY EASY! 2¹/₄ HOURS SERVES 6

2 teaspoons cumin seeds

2 teaspoons black mustard seeds

1 teaspoon cardamom seeds

1 teaspoon ground turmeric

1 teaspoon ground cinnamon

1/2 teaspoon black peppercorns

6 whole cloves

5 small dried red chillies

4 tablespoons white vinegar

1 tablespoon soft brown sugar

4 tablespoons oil

1 large onion, chopped

6–8 garlic cloves, crushed

1 tablespoon finely grated ginger

1.5 kg (3 lb 5 oz) pork leg, cut into 3 cm (1 inch) cubes

When using cardamom seeds, the easiest way to get the seeds out of the pods is to crush the pods with the blade of a heavy knife and remove the seeds with your fingers.

Dry-fry the spices and chillies in a large frying pan for 2 minutes, or until fragrant. Grind finely in a food processor. Place in a bowl and stir in vinegar, sugar and 1 teaspoon salt to make a paste.

Heat half the oil in a large saucepan. Add chopped onion and cook for 5 minutes, or until golden. Place onion in a food processor with 2 tablespoons cold water. Process until smooth. Stir into spice paste.

Place the garlic and ginger in a small bowl, mix together well and stir in 2 tablespoons water.

Heat remaining oil in pan over high heat. Add the cubed pork and cook in 3–4 batches for 8 minutes, or until well browned. Return all the meat to the pan and stir in garlic and ginger mixture. Add the onion mixture along with 250 ml (9 fl oz/1 cup) hot water. Simmer, covered, for 1 hour, or until pork is tender. Uncover, bring to the boil and cook, stirring frequently, for 10 minutes, or until sauce reduces and thickens slightly.

EASY!   2¼ HOURS   SERVES 6

SRI LANKAN PORK AND TAMARIND CURRY

Serve this curry with cucumber raita (page 213) or aubergine sambal (page 233).

Heat the oil in a heavy-based Dutch oven or a deep, lidded frying pan. Add onion, garlic, curry powder, ginger, curry leaves, chilli powder, 1 teaspoon salt and fenugreek and cook, stirring, over medium heat for 5 minutes.

Add pork, lemongrass, tamarind purée, cardamom and 375 ml (13 fl oz/1¹/₂ cups) hot water, then reduce the heat and simmer, covered, for 1 hour.

Stir in the coconut cream and simmer, uncovered, for 40–45 minutes, or until the sauce has reduced and become thick and creamy.

REALLY EASY! · 2¹/₄ HOURS · SERVES 6

4 tablespoons oil

2 onions, thickly sliced

4 large garlic cloves, crushed

3 tablespoons Sri Lankan curry powder (page 39)

1 tablespoon grated ginger

10 dried curry leaves or 5 fresh curry leaves

2 teaspoons chilli powder

¹/₄ teaspoon fenugreek seeds

1.25 kg (2 lb 12 oz) lean shoulder pork, cubed

1 lemongrass stem, white part only, finely chopped

2 tablespoons tamarind purée

4 cardamom pods, crushed

400 ml (14 fl oz) coconut cream

FIVE-SPICE PORK CURRY

500 g (1 lb 2 oz) pork
spare ribs

1 1/2 tablespoons oil

2 garlic cloves, crushed

190 g (6 3/4 oz) fried
tofu puffs

1 tablespoon finely
chopped ginger

1 teaspoon five-spice

1/2 teaspoon ground white
pepper

3 tablespoons fish sauce

3 tablespoons kecap manis

2 tablespoons light
soy sauce

3 tablespoons shaved
palm sugar (jaggery), or
soft brown sugar

1 small handful coriander
(cilantro) leaves, chopped

100 g (3 1/2 oz) snow peas
(mangetout), thinly sliced

This dish draws on various influences to create a spicy, salty and fragrant curry. Five-spice is widely used in many Asian countries besides China, and here it is mixed with kecap manis, a thick, sweet dark soy sauce from Indonesia. Five-spice has a strong flavour, so use sparingly.

Cut spare ribs into 2.5 cm (1 inch) thick pieces and discard any small pieces of bone. Put them into a saucepan and cover with cold water. Bring to the boil, reduce to a simmer and cook for 5 minutes. Drain and set aside.

Heat oil in a heavy-based saucepan over medium–high heat. Add the pork and garlic and stir until lightly browned. Add remaining ingredients except snow peas, plus 560 ml (19 1/4 fl oz/2 1/4 cups) water. Cover, bring to the boil then reduce to a simmer and cook, stirring occasionally, for 15–18 minutes, or until the pork is tender. Stir in the snow peas and serve.

REALLY EASY!

40 MINUTES

SERVES 4

HOT PORK CURRY WITH PUMPKIN

Garnish with sprigs of basil, if you like, and serve with steamed rice.

Heat the oil in a wok or heavy-based pan; add curry paste and stir for 1 minute. Add pork and stir-fry over medium–high heat until golden brown.

Add the coconut milk, 125ml (4 fl oz/½ cup) water, pumpkin and lime leaves, reduce heat and simmer for 20 minutes, or until the pork is tender.

Add the coconut cream, fish sauce and sugar to the wok and stir to combine. Scatter chilli over the top.

 REALLY EASY!

 45 MINUTES

SERVES 4

1 tablespoon oil

1–2 tablespoons red curry paste (page 31) or ready-made paste

500 g (1 lb 2 oz) lean pork, cut into thick strips or chunks

250 ml (9 fl oz/1 cup) coconut milk

350 g (12 oz) butternut pumpkin (squash), cut into small chunks

6 kaffir lime (makrut) leaves

3 tablespoons coconut cream

1 tablespoon fish sauce

1 teaspoon soft brown sugar

2 red chillies, thinly sliced

CURRY PASTE

10 cardamom pods

6 cm (2½ inch) piece ginger, chopped

3 garlic cloves, crushed

2 teaspoons black peppercorns

1 cinnamon stick

1 onion, thinly sliced

1 teaspoon ground cumin

1 teaspoon ground coriander

1 teaspoon garam masala (page 36)

3 tablespoons oil

1 kg (2 lb 4 oz) pork fillet, thinly sliced

2 tomatoes, finely diced

125 ml (4 fl oz/½ cup) chicken stock

125 ml (4 fl oz/½ cup) coconut milk

Tender, sweet pork fillet is perfect for this dish: it has no visible fat, so needs an initial brief cooking to seal in the juices, but then will cook fairly quickly in the curry. The spices — peppercorns, ginger, cardamom, cumin, garam masala — combine to give this dish a lovely warm, exotic flavour.

Crush the cardamom pods lightly with the flat side of a heavy knife. Remove the seeds, discarding the pods. Put the seeds and the remaining curry paste ingredients in a food processor, or in a mortar with a pestle, and process or pound to a smooth paste.

Put 2½ tablespoons of oil in a large heavy-based frying pan. Fry pork in batches until browned, then set aside. Add remaining oil to the pan, then add the curry paste and cook over medium–high heat for 3–4 minutes, or until aromatic. Add tomato, chicken stock and coconut milk, and simmer covered over a low–medium heat for 15 minutes. While cooking, skim any oil that comes to the surface and discard.

Add the pork to the sauce, and simmer uncovered for 5 minutes, or until cooked. Season well to taste.

EASY! 1 HOUR SERVES 6

CHIANG MAI PORK CURRY

CURRY PASTE

1 tablespoon coriander
seeds

2 teaspoons cumin seeds

2 dried long red chillies

5 cm (2 inch) piece
galangal, grated

1 lemongrass stem, white
part only, finely chopped

2 red Asian shallots,
chopped

2 garlic cloves, crushed

1/4 teaspoon ground
turmeric

1 teaspoon shrimp paste

1/2 teaspoon ground
cinnamon

Continued →

This Burmese-style curry is typical of the Chiang Mai area in Thailand's north. It is unlike the majority of fragrant Thai curries, in that it has a spicier, almost Indian flavour. Generally made with pork, you will occasionally find it made with chicken. This curry improves if made in advance.

Dry-fry the coriander and cumin seeds in a frying pan over medium–high heat for 2–3 minutes, or until fragrant. Allow to cool. Using a mortar with a pestle, or a spice grinder, crush or grind to a powder.

Soak chillies in boiling water for 5 minutes, or until soft. Remove the stem and seeds, then chop. Put the chillies, ground coriander and cumin seeds with the remaining curry paste ingredients and $1/2$ teaspoon salt in a food processor, or in a mortar with a pestle, and process or pound to a smooth paste. Add a little oil if it is too thick.

Blanch pork cubes in boiling water for 1 minute, then drain well. Heat the oil in a wok or saucepan and fry the garlic for 1 minute. Add 2 tablespoons of the made curry paste and stir-fry until fragrant. Add the shallots, ginger, peanuts and pork, and stir briefly. Add 500 ml (17 fl oz/2 cups) water and the tamarind purée and bring to the boil.

Add fish sauce and sugar and simmer for $1\frac{1}{4}$ hours, or until the pork is very tender. Add more water as the pork cooks, if necessary.

500 g (1 lb 2 oz) pork belly, cut into cubes

2 tablespoons oil

2 garlic cloves, crushed

4 red Asian shallots, crushed with the blade of a cleaver

3 teaspoons grated ginger

4 tablespoons toasted peanuts

3 tablespoons tamarind purée

2 tablespoons fish sauce

2 tablespoons shaved palm sugar (jaggery), or soft brown sugar

EASY! 1³/₄ HOURS SERVES 6

PORK CURRY WITH AUBERGINE

CURRY PASTE

4 long red chillies, split lengthways, seeded

1 slice galangal, chopped

1 spring onion (scallion), chopped

2 garlic cloves, chopped

2 coriander (cilantro) roots, chopped

1 lemongrass stem, white part only, thinly sliced

1 teaspoon ground white pepper

2 teaspoons fish sauce

2 tablespoons crunchy peanut butter

600 g (1 lb 5 oz) pork shoulder

2 tablespoons shaved palm sugar (jaggery)

4 tablespoons fish sauce

400 ml (14 fl oz) coconut cream (don't shake the tin)

250 g (9 oz) aubergine (eggplant), in small cubes

225 g (8 oz) tinned bamboo pieces, drained, sliced

Put split chillies in a shallow bowl and pour over enough hot water to just cover. Leave 15 minutes. Drain, reserving 1 tablespoon of the soaking liquid.

Place chillies and reserved soaking liquid with rest of curry paste ingredients, except the peanut butter, in a food processor and process to a smooth paste. Stir in peanut butter.

Cut pork into 1 cm ($^1/_2$ inch) thick slices. Put in a saucepan and cover with water. Add 1 tablespoon palm sugar and fish sauce. Bring to the boil over high heat, then simmer for 25 minutes, or until meat is tender. Remove from heat and cool meat in stock. Strain; reserve 250 ml (9 fl oz/1 cup) of liquid.

Scoop coconut cream from top of tin into a pan, bring to a rapid simmer over medium heat, stirring occasionally. Cook for 5–10 minutes, or until the oil starts to separate. Add curry paste and remaining palm sugar and fish sauce; bring to the boil. Then simmer 3 minutes, or until fragrant. Add pork, aubergine, sliced bamboo, reserved pork cooking liquid and remaining coconut cream. Increase heat; bring to a boil. Then simmer for 20 minutes, or until aubergine is tender and sauce is slightly thickened.

EASY! · 1 3/4 HOURS · SERVES 4

INDIAN PORK, HONEY AND ALMOND CURRY

This unusual curry blends aromatic cinnamon and cardamom with sweet honey and almonds, fragrant citrus and the fresh liveliness of parsley and coriander. Pork is the perfect choice for this mix of aromas and flavours, complementing rather than being swamped by them.

Dry-fry the cinnamon and cardamom in a frying pan over medium–high heat for 2–3 minutes, or until fragrant. Allow to cool. Using a mortar with a pestle, or a spice grinder, crush to a powder.

Cut the pork into 2 cm (³/₄ inch) cubes. Heat the oil and honey in a heavy-based saucepan over medium heat. Add the cubed pork, garlic and onion and then cook for 8–10 minutes, or until onion is translucent and pork light golden. Add 200 ml (7 fl oz) water and the chicken stock, bring to the boil then reduce to a simmer, cover and cook, stirring occasionally, for 1¼ hours, or until the pork is tender.

Uncover and then simmer rapidly for 10 minutes, or until most of the liquid is absorbed. Add the crushed spices, turmeric, pepper, 1 teaspoon salt and citrus zest and simmer for 3–4 minutes. To serve, gently stir in yoghurt, almonds, chopped coriander and parsley.

1 cinnamon stick

3 cardamom pods

750 g (1 lb 10 oz) boneless pork shoulder

1 tablespoon oil

2 tablespoons honey

3 garlic cloves, crushed

2 onions, chopped

150 ml (5 fl oz) chicken stock

1 teaspoon ground turmeric

¹/₂ teaspoon ground black pepper

1 teaspoon each grated lemon and orange zest

250 g (9 oz/1 cup) plain yoghurt

3 tablespoons slivered almonds, toasted

1 small handful each coriander (cilantro) and parsley leaves, chopped

EASY! **2** HOURS SERVES **4**

9 thick pork sausages

1 tablespoon vegetable oil

20 g ($^3/_4$ oz) butter

2 teaspoons grated ginger

3 garlic cloves, crushed

2 large onions, sliced

3 teaspoons curry powder

1 teaspoon garam masala (page 36)

2 teaspoons tomato paste (concentrated purée)

1 tablespoon plain (all-purpose) flour

625 ml (21$^1/_2$ fl oz/ 2$^1/_2$ cups) hot chicken stock

2 bay leaves

This is an easy and inexpensive dish but try to find reasonably good quality sausages. They will make a big difference to the flavour.

Place the sausages in a saucepan, cover with cold water and bring to the boil. Reduce heat and simmer for 3 minutes. Remove from the heat and allow the sausages to cool in the water, then drain, pat dry, and cut into 2 cm ($^3/_4$ inch) pieces.

Heat the oil in a large frying pan over high heat and cook the sausages for 2–3 minutes, or until golden all over. Drain on paper towels.

Melt the butter in the same pan, then add the ginger, garlic and onion. Cook over medium heat for about 5 minutes, or until the onion is soft and golden. Add curry powder and garam masala and cook for 1 minute, or until fragrant. Stir in tomato paste and cook for 1 minute, then add flour. Stir to combine, then gradually pour in stock, taking care that no lumps form. Bring to a simmer, add the bay leaves and the sausages and cook over low heat for 15 minutes, or until thickened. Season and then serve with mashed potato.

REALLY EASY!   45 MINUTES   SERVES 6

SWEET KECAP PORK

Serve this with plenty of steamed rice and, if you fancy a bit of extra heat, some fresh chopped chilli.

Mix together the pork, oil and $\frac{1}{4}$ teaspoon each of salt and pepper. Heat a wok or heavy-based pan and cook the pork in several batches over medium heat, until well browned. Remove all the meat from the wok and set aside.

Reduce the heat to low; add the onion, garlic, ginger and chilli and cook for 10 minutes, stirring occasionally, until the onion is very soft and golden.

Add the pork, kecap manis and coconut milk, and cook over low heat for 1 hour, stirring occasionally. Stir in the lime juice.

500 g (1 lb 2 oz) diced pork

2 tablespoons oil

1 large onion, finely chopped

3 garlic cloves, finely chopped

5 cm (2 inch) piece ginger, grated

3 red chillies, finely chopped

2 tablespoons kecap manis

250 ml (9 fl oz/1 cup) coconut milk

2 teaspoons lime juice

GREEN HERB PORK CURRY

The use of coriander and dill, mixed with yoghurt gives this dish a fresh burst of flavour.

Dry-fry the coriander and fennel seeds in a frying pan over medium–high heat for 2–3 minutes, or until fragrant. Allow to cool. Using a large mortar with a pestle, or a spice grinder, grind to a powder. Add pepper, ginger, garlic and onion and mix to a smooth paste. Add a little water if it is too thick.

Heat 2 tablespoons of the oil in a heavy-based saucepan over high heat, and brown the pork in batches. Set aside. Reduce the heat to low, add rest of oil, and cook spice and onion paste, stirring constantly, for 5–8 minutes. Return the pork to the pan, and stir to coat with paste. Add chicken stock, increase heat to high and bring to boil then reduce to a slow simmer, cover and cook for 2–2^1/$_2$ hours, or until pork is tender. While cooking, stir and skim any oil that comes to the surface and discard.

Put the yoghurt, chopped coriander, dill and about 3 tablespoons of pork cooking liquid in a jug or bowl and blend with a stick blender until smooth, then add back into the pork. Remove heat; season..

2 teaspoons coriander seeds

2 teaspoons fennel seeds

1/4 teaspoon ground white pepper

1^1/$_2$ tablespoons grated ginger

6 garlic cloves, crushed

2 onions, chopped

3 tablespoons oil

1 kg (2 lb 4 oz) pork shoulder, cut into 2 cm (3/4 inch) dice

250 ml (9 fl oz/1 cup) chicken stock

125 g (4^1/$_2$ oz/^{1}/$_2$ cup) plain yoghurt

1 large handful coriander (cilantro) leaves, roughly chopped

1 large handful dill, roughly chopped

EASY!   3^1/$_4$ HOURS   SERVES 6

CHICKEN & DUCK

POULTRY

Cuts of chicken on the bone are often used for curries because they can withstand the longer cooking times of braising. Other cuts, such as chicken breast are usually reserved for when the cooking time is shorter. Chinese barbecued duck is an easy ingredient to use because it is already cooked and needs only a short cooking time before it is ready to eat.

BALTI CHICKEN

A balti is traditionally cooked and served in a balti, a distinctive, round-bottomed, wok-like, cast-iron pan with two handles.

Cut the chicken into 3 cm (1¼ inch) cubes.

Heat the ghee in a balti pan or wok; stir-fry the garlic, cinnamon stick, cardamom seeds and the garam masala over medium heat for 1 minute. Add the sesame, poppy and fennel seeds, and fry for a further for 30 seconds. Reduce the heat, add onion and cook for 10 minutes or until the onion is soft and golden brown.

Add the masala paste and chicken and cook, stirring occasionally, for 5 minutes.

Reduce heat and add stock. Cover and simmer for 20 minutes. Add the cream and cook for a further 10 minutes, stirring occasionally.

Stir in the coriander leaves, and season with salt and pepper to taste.

1 kg (2 lb 4 oz) boneless, skinless chicken thighs

2 tablespoons ghee or oil

2 garlic cloves, crushed

1 cinnamon stick

½ teaspoon cardamom seeds

1 tablespoon garam masala (page 36)

1 teaspoon sesame seeds

1 teaspoon poppy seeds

½ teaspoon fennel seeds

2 onions, thinly sliced

3 tablespoons balti masala paste (page 25)

250 ml (9 fl oz/1 cup) chicken stock

250 ml (9 fl oz/1 cup) cream

1 tablespoon coriander (cilantro) leaves

REALLY EASY!　　1 HOUR　　SERVES 4

SPICED CHICKEN WITH ALMONDS

3 tablespoons oil

3 tablespoons slivered almonds

2 red onions, finely chopped

4–6 garlic cloves, crushed

1 tablespoon grated ginger

4 cardamom pods, bruised

4 cloves

1 teaspoon ground cumin

1 teaspoon ground coriander

1 teaspoon ground turmeric

$1/2$ teaspoon chilli powder

1 kg (2 lb 4 oz) boneless, skinless chicken thighs

2 large tomatoes, peeled, chopped

1 cinnamon stick

100 g ($3^1/2$ oz/1 cup) ground almonds

This is a wonderfully simple and aromatic dish, with little of the spiciness found in many curries.

Heat 1 tablespoon oil in a large saucepan. Add the almonds and cook over low heat for 15 seconds, or until lightly golden brown. Remove and drain on crumpled paper towels.

Heat the remaining oil, add the onion and cook, stirring, for 8 minutes, or until golden brown. Add garlic and ginger and cook, stirring, for 2 minutes, then stir in the spices. Reduce the heat to low and cook for 2 minutes, or until aromatic.

Add the chicken and cook, stirring constantly, for 5 minutes, or until well coated with spices and starting to colour.

Stir in the tomato, cinnamon stick, ground almonds and 250 ml (9 fl oz/1 cup) hot water. Simmer over low heat, covered, for 1 hour, or until chicken is cooked through and tender. Stir often and add a little more water, if needed.

Leave the pan to stand, covered, for 30 minutes for the flavours to develop. Remove cinnamon stick. Scatter slivered almonds over the top and serve.

REALLY EASY! 2¼ HOURS SERVES 6

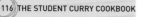

YELLOW CHICKEN PEPPERCORN CURRY

Fresh peppercorns have a fragrant quality that lifts the flavour of any curry in which they are used. You should beware of eating a whole sprig in one go though, as just like the pepper they become, they are extremely hot.

Put the coconut cream in a wok or saucepan and simmer over medium heat for about 5 minutes, or until the cream separates and a layer of oil forms on the surface. Stir the cream if ichicken curry starts to brown around the edges.

Stir in the curry paste until combined and cook until fragrant. Add the fish sauce, palm sugar and turmeric and stir well. Cook for 2–3 minutes, stirring occasionally, until the mixture darkens.

Add the chicken to the pan and stir to coat all the pieces evenly in the spice mixture. Cook over medium heat for 5 minutes, stirring occasionally and adding coconut milk a tablespoon at a time. Add bamboo shoots, peppercorns, lime and basil leaves and cook for another 5 minutes.

3 tablespoons coconut cream

2 tablespoons yellow curry paste (page 34)

1 tablespoon fish sauce

2 teaspoons palm sugar (jaggery), or soft brown sugar

1/4 teaspoon ground turmeric

600 g (1 lb 5 oz) boneless, skinless chicken thighs, cut into thin slices

440 ml (15 1/4 fl oz/ 1 3/4 cups) coconut milk

100 g (3 1/2 oz) tinned bamboo pieces, drained, thinly sliced

4 sprigs fresh green peppercorns

4–6 kaffir lime (makrut) leaves

12 Thai sweet basil leaves

MALAY
COCON

1.6 kg (3^1/$_2$ lb) chicken pieces

----

1 tablespoon oil

----

2 onions, sliced

----

3 garlic cloves, crushed

----

2 red chillies, seeded, chopped

----

45 g (1^1/$_2$ oz/^{1}/$_2$ cup) desiccated coconut

----

2 teaspoons ground turmeric

----

2 teaspoons ground coriander

----

2 teaspoons ground cumin

----

2 lemongrass stems, white part only, chopped

----

8 curry leaves

----

500 ml (17 fl oz/2 cups) coconut milk

This is ideal if you have very little time to spend in the kitchen. It virtually takes care of itself.

Heat the oil in a large pan and cook the onion until soft. Add the garlic, chilli, coconut and turmeric. Stir mixture for 1 minute. Add the coriander, cumin, lemongrass, curry leaves and coconut milk. Stir until well combined.

Add the chicken pieces and stir until well coated with the sauce. Simmer, uncovered, 45–60 minutes, or until chicken is tender and sauce has thickened.

REALLY EASY!　1^1/$_4$ HOURS　SERVES 4-6

INDONESIAN CHICKEN IN COCONUT MILK

This heady dish perfectly conjures Indonesia's tropical climate and produce. Curries are typically rich, relying on ingredients such as pepper, shrimp paste, galangal and coriander for hot, tangy, sharp and salty elements. Nutmeg, although native to the area, is a surprisingly rare curry addition.

Dry-fry the coriander seeds, cumin seeds, white peppercorns and shrimp paste, wrapped in some foil, in a frying pan over medium–high heat for 2–3 minutes, or until fragrant. Allow to cool. Using a mortar with a pestle, or a spice grinder, crush or grind the coriander, cumin and peppercorns to a powder. Process the shrimp in a food processor until it is very finely shredded — forming a 'floss'.

Put crushed spices, shrimp and remaining paste ingredients in a food processor, or a mortar with a pestle, and process or pound to a smooth paste.

Heat a large saucepan or wok over medium heat, add the coconut cream and curry paste, and cook, stirring, for 20 minutes, or until thick and oily.

Add the chicken and the remaining ingredients and simmer gently for 50 minutes, or until the chicken is tender. Season to taste and serve immediately.

CURRY PASTE

2 teaspoons coriander seeds

$\frac{1}{2}$ teaspoon cumin seeds

2 teaspoons white peppercorns

$\frac{1}{2}$ teaspoon shrimp paste

2 lemongrass stems, white part only, sliced

2 red onions, chopped

3 garlic cloves, crushed

1 tablespoon grated ginger

$2\frac{1}{2}$ tablespoons grated galangal

$\frac{1}{2}$ teaspoon ground nutmeg

---

560 ml (19$\frac{1}{4}$ fl oz/ 2$\frac{1}{4}$ cups) coconut cream

1.5 kg (3 lb 5 oz) chicken, cut into 8–10 pieces

800 ml (28 fl oz/3$\frac{1}{4}$ cups) coconut milk

2 tablespoons tamarind purée

1 tablespoon white vinegar

1 cinnamon stick

EASY!   1$\frac{1}{4}$ HOURS   SERVES 6

MALAYSIAN CHICKEN CURRY

3 teaspoons dried shrimp

4 tablespoons oil

6–8 red chillies, seeded, finely chopped

4 garlic cloves, crushed

3 lemongrass stems, white part only, finely chopped

2 teaspoons ground turmeric

10 candlenuts (see Note)

2 large onions, chopped

250 ml (9 fl oz/1 cup) coconut milk

1.5 kg (3 lb 5 oz) whole chicken, cut into 8 pieces

125 ml (4 fl oz/½ cup) coconut cream

2 tablespoons lime juice

Dry-fry shrimp in a frying pan over low heat, shaking pan regularly, for 3 minutes, until shrimp are dark orange and give off a strong aroma. Cool.

Put shrimp, half the oil, chilli, garlic, lemongrass, turmeric and candlenuts in a food processor, or in a mortar with a pestle. Process to a smooth paste.

Heat remaining oil in a frying pan, add onion and ¼ teaspoon salt. Cook over low–medium heat for 8 minutes, or until golden. Add spice paste and stir for 5 minutes. If mixture begins to stick to the pan, add 2 tablespoons coconut milk.

Add chicken to pan. Cook, stirring, for 5 minutes, or until it begins to brown. Stir in remaining coconut milk and 250 ml (9 fl oz/1 cup) water. Bring to the boil. Reduce the heat and simmer for 50 minutes, or until chicken is cooked and sauce has thickened slightly. Add the coconut cream and bring mixture back to the boil, stirring constantly. Add lime juice and serve immediately.

Note: Candlenuts must be cooked before being eaten as they are mildly toxic when raw.

EASY! · 1½ HOURS · SERVES 4–6

CHICKEN AND PEANUT PENANG CURRY

Penang curry paste is based on ground nuts (most often peanuts). Penang curry originated in Malaysia but now features in Thai and Indonesian cuisines. This is good with sliced cucumber and chilli sauce.

Heat the oil in a wok or large frying pan; add the onion and curry paste and stir over medium heat for 2 minutes. Add the coconut milk and bring to the boil.

Add chicken and lime leaves to the wok; reduce the heat and cook for 15 minutes. Remove the chicken with a wire mesh strainer or slotted spoon. Simmer the sauce for 5 minutes or until it is reduced and quite thick.

Return chicken to the wok. Add coconut cream, fish sauce, lime juice and sugar and cook for 5 minutes. Stir in the peanuts, basil and pineapple.

REALLY EASY! 45 MINUTES SERVES 4

1 tablespoon oil

1 large red onion, chopped

1–2 tablespoons penang curry paste (page 30)

250 ml (9 fl oz/1 cup) coconut milk

500 g (1 lb 2 oz) boneless, skinless chicken thighs, cut into bite-sized pieces

4 kaffir lime (makrut) leaves

3 tablespoons coconut cream

1 tablespoon fish sauce

1 tablespoon lime juice

2 teaspoons soft brown sugar

80 g (2^3/4 oz/^{1}/2 cup) toasted peanuts, chopped

2 large handfuls Thai basil leaves

80 g (2^3/4 oz/^{1}/2 cup) chopped pineapple

CHICKEN CURRY

1 kg (2 lb 4 oz) chicken thigh cutlets

2 large onions, roughly chopped

3 large garlic cloves, roughly chopped

5 cm (2 inch) piece ginger, roughly chopped

2 tablespoons peanut oil

$1/2$ teaspoon shrimp paste

500 ml (17 fl oz/2 cups) coconut milk

200 g (7 oz) dried rice vermicelli

ACCOMPANIMENTS

6 spring onions (scallions) diagonally sliced

4 tablespoons chopped coriander (cilantro) leaves

4 tablespoons garlic flakes, lightly fried

3 lemons, cut in wedges

12 dried chillies, fried in oil to crisp

125 ml (4 fl oz/$1/2$ cup) fish sauce

Chicken curry is a popular dish commonly served around the world. With this curry, diners can use the accompaniments to create as hot or as tart a flavour as they wish.

Wash the chicken under cold water and pat dry with paper towels.

Place onion, garlic and ginger in a food processor and process until smooth. Add a little water to help blend the mixture if necessary.

Heat oil in a large pan; add the onion mixture and shrimp paste and cook, stirring, over high heat for 5 minutes. Add chicken and cook over medium heat, turning it until it browns. Add 1 teaspoon salt and the coconut milk. Bring to the boil, reduce heat and simmer, covered, for 30 minutes, stirring the mixture occasionally. Uncover the pan and cook for 15 minutes, or until chicken is tender.

Put the noodles in a heatproof bowl, cover with boiling water and leave for 10 minutes. Drain the noodles and place them in a serving bowl.

Place accompaniments in separate bowls. Diners help themselves to some, or all, of them.

REALLY EASY!

1$1/4$ HOURS

SERVES 6

TANDOORI CHICKEN

Tandoori chicken is traditionally cooked over hot coals in a special clay oven called a tandoor. Some skill is required to ensure that the food does not burn. Fortunately, baking this recipe in a conventional oven also gives a delicious result.

Preheat oven to 180°C (350°F/Gas 4). Remove skin from chicken and brush flesh with lemon juice; set aside for 30 minutes to marinate.

Place onion, garlic, ginger, coriander and cumin seeds, extra lemon juice and 1 teaspoon salt in the small bowl of a food processor. Process until the mixture forms a smooth paste. Combine the spice paste with paprika, chilli powder and yoghurt and mix together until smooth. Add several drops of food colouring until the mixture is a deep red.

Lay out the chicken pieces in a large shallow dish. Spread liberally with the spice yoghurt mixture. Cover with plastic wrap and refrigerate. Marinate the chicken for several hours or overnight.

Place the chicken pieces on a wire rack over a large baking dish. Bake for 45 minutes, or until chicken pieces are tender and cooked through.

6 chicken thigh cutlets

3 tablespoons lemon juice

1/2 small onion, chopped

4 garlic cloves

1 tablespoon grated ginger

3 teaspoons coriander seeds

1 tablespoon cumin seeds

1 tablespoon lemon juice, extra

1/4 teaspoon paprika

pinch chilli powder

250 g (9 oz/1 cup) plain yoghurt

red food colouring

EASY!

1 HOUR + MARINATING TIME

SERVES 4-6

CHICKEN & DUCK 123

750 g (1 lb 10 oz) boned chicken thighs

----

3 tablespoons ghee or oil

----

1 large onion, halved and thinly sliced

----

1 teaspoon crushed garlic

1¹/₂ teaspoons grated ginger

----

1 cinnamon stick

----

2 dried chillies

----

2 bay leaves

----

2 cloves

----

seeds from 2 cardamom pods

----

1 tablespoon ground coriander

----

2 teaspoons garam masala (page 36)

----

¹/₂ teaspoon ground turmeric

----

lemon juice

This is a super-easy version of chicken curry, and is a perfect dinner option for nights when you need to focus on your studies, instead of cooking. It is simple but still delicious.

Brown the chicken pieces in ghee or oil, remove and set aside

Fry the onion until golden brown, add the garlic, ginger, cinnamon and chillies and fry for 2 minutes, stirring. Add spices and pepper.

Return the chicken and add water to barely cover. Cover the pan and simmer for about 40 minutes until the chicken is tender.

Add lemon juice to taste. Serve with rice and a tart-sweet chutney.

REALLY EASY! · 1 HOUR · SERVES 4

GREEN CHICKEN CURRY

This is a Thai curry that is both very hot and very sweet in flavour. You can substitute meat, fish or extra vegetables for the chicken. Serve with rice.

Put a wok over low heat, add the coconut cream and let it come to the boil. Stir it for a while until the oil separates out. Don't let it burn.

Add the green curry paste, stir for a minute, then add the chicken. Cook the chicken until it turns opaque, then add the coconut milk and aubergine. Cook for a minute or two until the aubergine is tender. Add the sugar, fish sauce, lime leaves and half of the basil, then mix together.

Garnish with the rest of the basil, the chilli and a drizzle of coconut milk or cream.

REALLY EASY! 30 MINUTES SERVES 4

250 ml (9 fl oz/1 cup) coconut cream

4 tablespoons green curry paste (page 27)

8 skinless chicken thighs or 4 chicken breasts, cut into pieces

250 ml (9 fl oz/1 cup) coconut milk

4 Thai aubergines (eggplants) or 1/2 of a purple aubergine, cut into chunks

2 tablespoons shaved palm sugar (jaggery), or soft brown sugar

2 tablespoons fish sauce

4 kaffir lime (makrut) leaves, torn

1 handful Thai basil leaves

1–2 large red chillies, sliced

coconut milk or cream, for drizzling

CREAMY CHICKEN CURRY

1 kg (2 lb 4 oz) chicken pieces

4 tablespoons ghee or vegetable oil

1 onion, quartered

2 garlic cloves

1 cm (1/2 inch) piece ginger

4 tablespoons ground almonds

1/2 teaspoon ground turmeric

1 teaspoon chilli powder

2 teaspoons ground cinnamon

250 ml (9 fl oz/1 cup) cream or coconut cream

1 1/2 teaspoons garam masala (page 36)

3 hard-boiled eggs

Serve this curry with a garnish of toasted flaked almonds, some lime wedges and a sprinkling of coriander leaves.

Cut the chicken pieces into 5 cm (2 inch) pieces with a cleaver or heavy knife. Brown in ghee or oil until evenly coloured, then remove and keep warm.

Grind the onion, garlic and ginger to a paste in a food processor or mortar with a pestle.

Fry in the same pan until golden. Add the ground almonds, turmeric, chilli and cinnamon. Cook for 1–2 minutes, stirring.

Return chicken to the pan with 250 ml (9 fl oz/1 cup) water. Partially cover and simmer until the chicken is tender, about 25 minutes, turning several times.

Stir in the cream, garam masala and hard-boiled eggs, cut into wedges. Heat through gently.

EASY! 55 MINUTES SERVES 6

NONYA CHICKEN AND LIME CURRY

Nonya cooking is a unique blend of Chinese ingredients and wok techniques, combined with Malay and Indonesian spices. It is tangy, aromatic, spicy and herbal.

To make the spice paste, place the onion, chilli, garlic, lemongrass, galangal and turmeric in a food processor and process for a few minutes until a thick rough paste is formed.

Heat oil in a large heavy-based pan and add spice paste. Cook over low heat for about 10 minutes, or until the paste is fragrant.

Add the chicken and stir-fry for 2 minutes, making sure it is covered with paste. Add the coconut milk, lime halves and shredded leaves; cover and simmer for about 50 minutes, or until chicken is tender. For the last 10 minutes of cooking, remove the lid and allow the cooking liquid to reduce until it is thick and creamy.

EASY!   1½ HOURS   SERVES 4

SPICE PASTE

1 large onion, roughly chopped

6 red chillies, seeded, finely chopped

4 garlic cloves, crushed

1 teaspoon finely chopped lemongrass, white part only

2 teaspoons finely chopped galangal

1 teaspoon ground turmeric

3 tablespoons oil

1.3 kg (3 lb) chicken pieces, skin removed

250 ml (9 fl oz/1 cup) coconut milk

2 limes, halved

5 kaffir lime (makrut) leaves, stems removed, finely shredded

CHICKEN CURRY WITH APRICOTS

18 dried apricots

1 tablespoon ghee

2 x 1.5 kg (3 lb 5 oz) chickens, jointed

3 onions, thinly sliced

1 teaspoon grated ginger

3 garlic cloves, crushed

3 large green chillies, seeded, finely chopped

1 teaspoon cumin seeds

1 teaspoon chilli powder

$^1/_2$ teaspoon ground turmeric

4 cardamom pods, bruised

4 large tomatoes, peeled, cut into eighths

Serve this curry with steamed rice mixed with raisins, grated carrot and toasted flaked almonds.

Soak the dried apricots in 250 ml (9 fl oz/1 cup) hot water for 1 hour.

Melt ghee in a large saucepan, add the chicken in batches and cook over high heat for 5–6 minutes, or until browned. Remove from pan. Add the onion and cook, stirring often, for 10 minutes, or until the onion has softened and turned golden brown.

Add ginger, garlic and chopped green chilli, and cook, stirring, for 2 minutes. Stir in cumin seeds, chilli powder and ground turmeric, and cook for a further 1 minute.

Return the chicken to the pan, add the cardamom, tomato and apricots, with any remaining liquid, and mix well. Simmer, covered, for 35 minutes, or until the chicken is tender.

Remove the chicken, cover and keep warm. Bring the liquid to the boil and boil rapidly, uncovered, for 5 minutes, or until it has thickened slightly. Spoon the liquid over the chicken.

EASY! · 1¼ HOURS + SOAKING TIME · SERVES 6-8

Ready-made peanut butter is a useful ingredient to have in the kitchen cupboard. In curries, it adds instant flavour and texture.

Put chicken pieces in a saucepan with the coconut cream and 250 ml (9 fl oz/1 cup) water. Add green chillies. Bring to the boil, cover and reduce heat. Simmer for 30 minutes until the chicken is tender.

Roast coriander, cumin, chilli flakes and shrimp paste in a dry wok or non-stick pan until very aromatic. Grind to a paste with the garlic, ginger and sugar.

Cook the seasoning paste in the oil for 2–3 minutes. Remove chicken with a slotted spoon and put aside. Pour the liquid, with chillies, over the seasonings. Simmer gently until the oil separates and the liquid is well reduced, about 20 minutes.

Add the peanut butter, stirring until dissolved into the sauce. Return the chicken and cook gently for 10 minutes. Add fish sauce and lime juice to taste.

1.5 kg (3 lb 5 oz) chicken pieces

400 ml (14 fl oz) coconut cream

2 green chillies, seeded, roughly chopped

2 tablespoons coriander seeds

1 teaspoon cumin seeds

1–2 teaspoons chilli flakes

1 teaspoon shrimp paste

1 teaspoon chopped garlic

1 teaspoon chopped ginger

2 teaspoons sugar

2 tablespoons oil

3 tablespoons crunchy peanut butter

2 tablespoons fish sauce

juice of 2 limes

EASY!

1½ HOURS

SERVES 6-8

BURMESE CHICKEN

2 tablespoons ghee or oil

2 onions, chopped

3 bay leaves

2 teaspoons ground turmeric

1/4 teaspoon chilli powder

1/2 teaspoon ground cardamom

1/2 teaspoon ground cumin

1/2 teaspoon ground coriander

1/2 teaspoon ground ginger

1 cinnamon stick

2 lemongrass stems, white part only, chopped

6 garlic cloves, crushed

1 tablespoon grated ginger

1.5 kg (3 lb/5 oz) chicken pieces

250 ml (9 fl oz/1 cup) chicken stock

Burmese cuisine is a fusion of traditional Burmese dishes and cooking methods, with Indian, Thai and Chinese influences. This dish is best served with basmati rice.

Heat the ghee in a large pan; add the onion and cook, stirring, until the onion is soft. Add the bay leaves, turmeric, chilli powder, cardamom, cumin, coriander, ginger, cinnamon stick, lemongrass, garlic and ginger. Cook, stirring, for 1 minute or until fragrant.

Add the chicken pieces and stir to coat with the mixture. Stir in the stock and simmer, covered, for 45 minutes to 1 hour or until the chicken is tender.

REALLY EASY!   1 1/4 HOURS   SERVES 4-6

OKRA CURRY WITH CHICKEN

Okra features in the cooking of many African, Asian and Caribbean countries, where it is valued for its flavour as well as for the mucilage it contains. This gluey liquid is released when the flesh is cut, and acts as a thickening agent in stews and soups. Serve this curry with boiled rice or a flat bread such as puri or chapatti.

Grind chilli flakes, turmeric, cumin, peppercorns and coconut in a spice mill or with a mortar and pestle until uniform.

Trim the okra by cutting off the tip and the tough stem end, being careful not to cut into the body.

Heat oil in a deep frying pan over medium heat. Fry onion and garlic for about 5 minutes, or until they are light brown. Stir in the spice mixture and fry for 1 minute. Add okra, chicken, tomato, sugar, coconut milk and chicken stock; bring to the boil.

Reduce the heat and simmer gently for 20 minutes. Add the vinegar and 1 teaspoon salt and simmer for 5 minutes. Check the seasoning.

1 teaspoon chilli flakes

$1/2$ teaspoon ground turmeric

$1/2$ teaspoon cumin seeds

4 white peppercorns

4 tablespoons desiccated coconut

500 g (1 lb 2 oz) okra

2 tablespoons oil

2 onions, sliced lengthways

3 garlic cloves, crushed

400 g (14 oz) boneless chicken thighs, trimmed, cut into quarters

1 large tomato, chopped

1 teaspoon sugar

250 ml (9 fl oz/1 cup) coconut milk

375 ml (13 fl oz/1$1/2$ cups) chicken stock

1 tablespoon malt vinegar

REALLY EASY! 45 MINUTES SERVES 4

CHICKEN KAPITAN

30 g (1 oz) small dried shrimp (prawns)

4 tablespoons oil

2 teaspoons ground turmeric

4–8 red chillies, seeded, finely chopped

4 garlic cloves, finely chopped

3 lemongrass stems, white part only, finely chopped

10 candlenuts (see Note)

2 large onions, chopped

1/4 teaspoon salt

250 ml (9 fl oz/1 cup) coconut milk

500 g (1 lb 2 oz) boneless chicken thighs, chopped

250 ml (9 fl oz/1 cup) water

125 ml (4 fl oz/1/2 cup) coconut cream

2 tablespoons lime juice

Dry-fry shrimp in a pan over low heat, shaking pan, for 3 minutes, or until shrimp are dark orange and give off a strong aroma. Transfer to a mortar and pestle and pound until finely ground. Set aside.

Place half the oil in a food processor with the turmeric, chilli, garlic, lemongrass and candlenuts and process until finely chopped, regularly scraping down the sides of the bowl

Heat remaining oil in wok or frying pan; add onion and salt and cook over low heat for 8 minutes, or until golden, stirring regularly. Add spice mixture and most of the ground shrimp, setting some aside to use as a garnish. Stir for 5 minutes. If mixture sticks to pan, add 2 tablespoons of coconut milk.

Add chicken to wok. Cook it for 5 minutes until it begins to brown. Stir in remaining coconut milk and water, and bring to the boil. Reduce heat and simmer for 7 minutes. Add coconut cream and bring mixture back to the boil, stirring constantly. Add lime juice and serve sprinkled lightly with the reserved ground shrimp meat and steamed rice.

Note: Raw candlenuts are mildly toxic and must be lightly cooked.

EASY!

1 HOUR

SERVES 6-8

BUTTER CHICKEN

2.5 cm (1 inch) piece ginger, roughly chopped

3 garlic cloves, roughly chopped

155 g (5$^{1}/_{2}$ oz/$^{1}/_{2}$ cup) blanched almonds

125 g (4$^{1}/_{2}$ oz/$^{1}/_{2}$ cup) plain yoghurt

$^{1}/_{2}$ teaspoon chilli powder

$^{1}/_{4}$ teaspoon ground cloves

$^{1}/_{4}$ teaspoon ground cinnamon

1 teaspoon garam masala (page 36)

4 cardamom pods, lightly crushed

400 g (14 oz) tin diced tomatoes

Continued →

Butter chicken, or murgh makhni, is a Moghul dish that has many versions. The butter in the title refers to ghee, a type of clarified butter. Rice is an ideal accompaniment and pieces of roti or naan can be used to mop up the delicious juices.

Blend the ginger and garlic to a paste in a food processor or mortar and pestle, or crush the garlic and finely grate ginger and mix them together. Grind the almonds in a food processor or finely chop with a knife. Put the paste and the almonds in a bowl with the yoghurt, chilli powder,

cloves, cinnamon, garam masala, cardamom pods, tomatoes and 1¼ teaspoons salt, and blend together with a fork. Add chicken pieces and stir to coat thoroughly. Cover and marinate for 2 hours, or overnight, in the fridge.

Preheat the oven to 180°C (350°F/Gas 4). Heat the ghee or clarified butter in a karhai or deep, heavy-bottomed frying pan, add the onion and fry until soft and brown. Add the chicken mixture and then fry for 2 minutes. Mix in the coriander. Put the mixture into a shallow baking dish, pour in the cream and stir with a fork.

Bake for 1 hour. If the top is browning too quickly during cooking, cover with a piece of aluminium foil. Allow to rest for 10 minutes before serving. The oil will rise to the surface. Just before serving, place the dish under a grill (broiler) for 2 minutes to brown the top. Before serving, slightly tip the dish and remove any extra oil with a spoon.

900 g (2 lb) skinless, boneless chicken thighs, cut into fairly large pieces

100 g (3½ oz) ghee or clarified butter

1 large onion, thinly sliced

6 tablespoons finely chopped coriander (cilantro) leaves

4 tablespoons thick (double/heavy) cream

EASY!

1½ HOURS + MARINATING TIME

SERVES 6

3 tablespoons oil

2 large onions, thinly sliced

1 garlic clove, finely chopped

5 cm (2 inch) piece ginger, finely chopped

3 dried chillies

1$\frac{1}{2}$ teaspoons garam masala (page 36)

1.3 kg (3 lb) chicken pieces

2 tablespoons tomato paste (concentrated purée)

2 tablespoons clear vinegar

1$\frac{1}{2}$ tablespoons palm sugar (jaggery) or soft brown sugar

12 dried apricots

In this delicious parsi dish from Mumbai (Bombay), the use of dried apricots, jaggery and vinegar give a sweet–sour flavour.

Heat the oil in a karhai or casserole. Add the onion and stir over medium heat until soft and starting to brown.

Stir in the garlic, ginger, dried chillies and garam masala, then add chicken pieces. Stir and brown the chicken for 5 minutes, taking care not to burn the onions.

Add the tomato paste, 1 teaspoon salt and 250 ml (9 fl oz/1 cup) water. Bring to the boil, then reduce the heat, cover and simmer gently for 20 minutes.

Add the vinegar, palm sugar and dried apricots to the pan, cover and simmer for another 15 minutes.

REALLY EASY!

1 HOUR

SERVES 4

SAFFRON CHICKEN

Saffron features in Indian, Iranian, Arab, Central Asian, European and Turkish cuisines. It is an expensive spice, because of the way it is harvested, but it can be bought in small, economical amounts.

Fry the saffron threads in a dry frying pan over low heat for 1–2 minutes. Transfer to a small bowl, add the hot water and set aside.

Heat the oil in a pan over medium heat; add the onion, garlic, ginger and chilli. Cover and cook for 10 minutes, or until very soft.

Add spices, and then cook over medium heat for 2 minutes. Add chicken and cook over high heat for 3 minutes, or until meat is well coated. Add the saffron liquid and the stock. Bring to the boil, then reduce the heat, and cook, covered, stirring occasionally, for 30 minutes.

Uncover, and cook for another 20 minutes. Remove chicken and keep warm. Reduce stock to around 375 ml (13 fl oz/1^1/$_2$ cups) over very high heat. Pour over chicken. Season with salt and pepper, to taste.

1 teaspoon saffron threads

2 tablespoons hot water

2 tablespoons oil

2 onions, chopped

3 garlic cloves, crushed

3 cm (1^1/$_4$ inch) piece ginger, chopped

2 red chillies, seeded, sliced

1 teaspoon ground cardamom

1 teaspoon ground cumin

^{1}/$_2$ teaspoon ground turmeric

2 kg (4 lb 8 oz) chicken pieces

500 ml (17 fl oz/2 cups) chicken stock

EASY!

1^3/$_4$ HOURS

SERVES 6

JAMAICAN CURRIED CHICKEN

60 g (2¼ oz) ghee or butter

2 tablespoons oil

1.5 kg (3 lb 5 oz) chicken pieces

1 tablespoon coconut vinegar

500 g (1 lb 2 oz) potatoes, cut into 4 cm (1½ inch) cubes

2 large onions, sliced

2 small red chillies, finely chopped

1 cinnamon stick

4 whole cloves

750 ml (26 fl oz/3 cups) chicken stock

3 tablespoons plain (all-purpose) flour

2½ tablespoons Indian curry powder

2 tablespoons dark brown sugar

½ teaspoon ground allspice (Jamaican pepper)

4 tablespoons lime juice

400 ml (14 fl oz) coconut milk

Serve the curry with basmati rice and aubergine sambal (page 233).

Heat the ghee and oil in a large saucepan or casserole dish. Cook the chicken pieces in batches over medium heat for 10 minutes, or until browned.

Stir in the vinegar and allow to boil and evaporate. Add the potato, onion, chilli, cinnamon and cloves, and cook, stirring, for 3 minutes. Pour in chicken stock and bring to the boil.

Place flour, curry powder, sugar and allspice in a small bowl. Pour in lime juice and stir to form a smooth paste. Stir paste into the chicken mixture.

Reduce the heat, add the coconut milk to the pan and simmer, covered, for 30–40 minutes, or until the chicken and potato are tender and the sauce has slightly thickened.

EASY! 1½ HOURS SERVES 6

SPICY CHICKEN AND TOMATO CURRY

This recipe contains spices that range from hot to sweet, and from sharp to gently perfumed.

Heat oil in a large frying pan over medium heat, add chicken in batches and cook for 5–10 minutes, or until browned, then transfer to a large saucepan.

Add onion to frying pan and cook, stirring, for 10–12 minutes, or until golden. Stir in the ground cloves, turmeric, garam masala and chilli powder, and cook, stirring, for 1 minute. Add to chicken.

Lightly crush cardamom pods with the flat side of a heavy knife. Remove seeds, discarding the pods. Put the seeds and the garlic, ginger, poppy seeds, fennel seeds and 2 tablespoons of coconut milk in a food processor, or in a mortar with a pestle, and process to a smooth paste. Add spice mixture, remaining coconut milk, star anise, the cinnamon stick, tomato and 3 tablespoons water to chicken.

Simmer, covered, for 45 minutes, or until chicken is tender. Remove chicken, cover and keep warm. Bring cooking liquid to the boil and boil for about 20–25 minutes, or until reduced by half. Place the chicken on a serving plate, mix the lime juice with the cooking liquid and pour over the chicken.

1 tablespoon oil

2 x 1.5 kg (3 lb 5 oz) chickens, jointed

1 onion, sliced

1/2 teaspoon ground cloves

1 teaspoon ground turmeric

2 teaspoons garam masala (page 36)

3 teaspoons chilli powder

3 cardamom pods

3 garlic cloves, crushed

1 tablespoon grated ginger

1 tablespoon poppy seeds

2 teaspoons fennel seeds

250 ml (9 fl oz/1 cup) coconut milk

1 star anise

1 cinnamon stick

4 large tomatoes, roughly chopped

2 tablespoons lime juice

REALLY EASY! · 2 HOURS · SERVES 8-10

6 cardamom pods

6 cloves

1 teaspoon cumin seeds

$1/2$ teaspoon cayenne pepper

2 tablespoons ghee or oil

1 kg (2 lb 4 oz) skinless, boneless chicken thighs, cut into 2.5 cm (1 inch) cubes

1 onion, finely chopped

3 garlic cloves, crushed

$1^{1}/2$ tablespoons finely grated ginger

2 cinnamon sticks

2 bay leaves

4 tablespoons blanched almonds, lightly toasted

4 tablespoons raisins

250 g (9 oz/1 cup) plain yoghurt

125 ml (4 fl oz/$^{1}/2$ cup) chicken stock

The dish features relatively few spices, but they are in perfect harmony with each other. The almonds and raisins add texture as well as flavour.

Crush cardamom pods lightly with the flat side of a heavy knife. Remove seeds, discarding the pods. Dry-fry seeds along with the cloves, cumin seeds and cayenne pepper in a frying pan over medium–high heat for 2–3 minutes, or until fragrant. Allow to cool. Using a mortar with a pestle, or a spice grinder, crush or grind to a powder.

Heat the ghee or oil in a large heavy-based frying pan over medium–high heat. Brown the chicken in batches and set aside. In the same pan, cook onion, garlic and ginger over low heat for 5–8 minutes or until soft. Add ground spice mix, cinnamon sticks and bay leaves, and cook, stirring constantly, for 5 minutes. Put almonds, raisins and chicken back into the pan. Add the yoghurt a spoonful at a time, stirring to incorporate it into the dish.

Add chicken stock, reduce heat to low, cover and then cook for 40 minutes, or until the chicken is tender. While cooking, skim any oil that comes to the surface and discard. Season well and serve.

EASY!   1$^{1}/2$ HOURS   SERVES 6

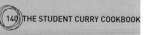

VIETNAMESE MILD CHICKEN CURRY

Remove skin and any excess fat from the chicken. Pat dry with paper towel and cut each quarter into 3 even pieces. Put curry powder, sugar, $^1/_2$ teaspoon black pepper and 2 teaspoons of salt in a bowl, and mix well. Rub curry mixture into the chicken pieces. Put them on a plate, cover with plastic wrap and refrigerate overnight.

Heat the oil in a large saucepan. Add sweet potato and cook over medium heat for 3 minutes, or until lightly golden. Remove with a slotted spoon.

Remove all but 2 tablespoons of oil from pan. Add onion and cook, stirring, for 5 minutes. Add garlic, lemongrass and bay leaves and cook for 2 minutes.

Add chicken and cook, stirring, over medium heat for 5 minutes, or until well coated and starting to change colour. Add 250 ml (9 fl oz/1 cup) water and and then simmer, covered, stirring occasionally, for 20 minutes.

Stir in carrot, sweet potato and coconut milk, and simmer, uncovered, stirring occasionally, for about 30 minutes, or until chicken is cooked and tender. Be careful not to break up the sweet potato cubes.

4 large chicken leg quarters

1 tablespoon Indian curry powder

1 teaspoon caster (superfine) sugar

4 tablespoons oil

500 g (1 lb 2 oz) sweet potato, cut into 3 cm (1$^1/_4$ inch) cubes

1 large onion, cut into thin wedges

4 garlic cloves, crushed

1 lemongrass stem, white part only, finely chopped

2 bay leaves

1 large carrot, cut into 1 cm ($^1/_2$ inch) pieces on the diagonal

400 ml (14 fl oz) coconut milk

EASY!

1$^1/_4$ HOURS + MARINATING TIME

SERVES 4

CHICKEN MASALA

1.5 kg (3 lb 5 oz) skinless, boneless chicken thighs or chicken pieces

2 teaspoons ground cumin

2 teaspoons ground coriander

$1\frac{1}{2}$ teaspoons garam masala (page 36)

$\frac{1}{4}$ teaspoon ground turmeric

2 onions, finely chopped

4 garlic cloves, roughly chopped

5 cm (2 inch) piece ginger, roughly chopped

2 ripe tomatoes, chopped

3 tablespoons ghee or oil

5 cloves

8 cardamom pods, bruised

1 cinnamon stick

10 curry leaves

160 g ($5\frac{3}{4}$ oz/$\frac{2}{3}$ cup) Greek-style yoghurt

Masala simply means 'mixture of spices', a catch-all word that could be used with just about any curry. In this case, the mixture is aromatic but only moderately spicy, giving the dish a subtle flavour.

Trim any excess fat from the chicken. Mix the cumin, coriander, garam masala and turmeric together and rub it into the chicken.

Put half the onion with garlic, ginger and chopped tomato in a food processor, or in a mortar with a pestle, and process or pound to a smooth paste.

Heat ghee or oil in a casserole dish over low heat, add remaining onion, cloves, cardamom, cinnamon and curry leaves and fry until onion is golden. Add the tomato and onion paste and stir for 5 minutes. Season with salt, to taste. Add yoghurt and whisk until smooth, then add spiced chicken. Toss pieces through and bring slowly to the boil.

Reduce the heat, cover and simmer for 50 minutes or until the oil separates from the sauce. Stir the ingredients occasionally to prevent chicken from sticking. If sauce is too thin, simmer for a couple of minutes with the lid off.

EASY! 1¼ HOURS SERVES 4

Dry-fry the coriander, cardamom, fenugreek and mustard seeds in a frying pan over medium–high heat for 2–3 minutes, or until fragrant. Cool. Using a spice grinder, or a mortar with a pestle, crush or grind spices with black peppercorns to a powder.

Put ground spices with the remaining curry paste ingredients in a food processor, or in a mortar with a pestle, and process or pound to a smooth paste.

Trim fat from duck fillets, then place, skin side down, in a large saucepan and cook over medium heat for 10 minutes, or until skin is brown and all fat has melted. Turn fillets over and cook for 5 minutes, or until tender. Remove and drain on paper towels.

Reserve 1 tablespoon duck fat, discard remaining fat. Add onion and cook for 5 minutes, then add the curry paste and stir over low heat for 10 minutes.

Return duck to pan and stir to coat with paste. Stir in the vinegar, coconut milk, 1 teaspoon salt and 125 ml (4 fl oz/$\frac{1}{2}$ cup) water. Simmer, covered, for 45 minutes, or until fillets are tender. If desired, stir in some coriander leaves just prior to serving.

CURRY PASTE

1$\frac{1}{2}$ teaspoons coriander seeds

1 teaspoon each of cardamom, fenugreek and brown mustard seeds

10 black peppercorns

1 red onion, chopped

2 garlic cloves, crushed

4 red chillies, seeded

2 coriander (cilantro) roots

2 teaspoons grated ginger

2 teaspoons garam masala

$\frac{1}{4}$ teaspoon turmeric

2 teaspoons tamarind

6 boneless duck breasts

1 red onion, sliced

125 ml (4 fl oz/$\frac{1}{2}$ cup) white vinegar

500 ml (17 fl oz/2 cups) coconut milk

THAI RED DUCK CURRY WITH PINEAPPLE

1 tablespoon peanut oil

8 spring onions (scallions), sliced on the diagonal into 2.5 cm (1 inch) lengths

2 garlic cloves, crushed

2–4 tablespoons red curry paste (page 31)

1 Chinese roast duck, chopped into large pieces

400 ml (14 fl oz) coconut milk

450 g (1 lb), tinned, drained pineapple pieces in syrup

3 kaffir lime (makrut) leaves

3 tablespoons chopped coriander (cilantro) leaves

2 tablespoons chopped mint

The art of Thai curries — and the reason why we keep coming back to them — is the way they combine different flavours and textures in the one dish to create an harmonious whole. This dish is a perfect example of it — blending sweet, savoury and spicy ingredients with rich coconut milk.

Heat a wok until very hot, add the oil and swirl to coat the side. Add the onion, garlic and curry paste, and stir-fry for 1 minute, or until fragrant.

Add the roast duck pieces, coconut milk, drained pineapple, kaffir lime leaves, and half the coriander and mint. Bring to the boil, then reduce heat and simmer for 10 minutes, or until the duck is heated through and sauce has thickened slightly. Stir in the remaining coriander and mint, and serve.

REALLY EASY! · 30 MINUTES · SERVES 4-6

QUICK DUCK CURRY

The Peking duck needed for this recipe is available from Chinese barbecue and roast meat outlets. Leave the skin on the duck if preferred. Serve this curry with jasmine rice or noodles.

Remove the skin and bones from the Peking duck and cut the meat into bite-size pieces.

Heat the oil in a saucepan over medium heat, add the onion and cook for 5 minutes. Add the garlic and chilli, and cook for 2 minutes. Stir in the curry paste and cook for 1–2 minutes, or until fragrant, then stir in the peanut butter.

Gradually whisk in coconut milk and then cook for 2 minutes, or until well combined. Add stock, bring to the boil, then reduce heat and simmer for 10 minutes. Add duck and simmer for 10 minutes. Stir in the lime juice and fish sauce. Scatter the coriander over the top.

REALLY EASY!

45 MINUTES

SERVES 4

1 kg (2 lb 4 oz) Peking duck

1 tablespoon oil

1 red onion, finely chopped

2 garlic cloves, crushed

1 red chilli, seeded, chopped

1 tablespoon red curry paste (page 31)

1 tablespoon smooth peanut butter

400 ml (14 fl oz) coconut milk

310 ml (10^{3}/$_{4}$ fl oz/ 1^{1}/$_{4}$ cups) chicken stock

1 tablespoon lime juice

1 tablespoon fish sauce

2 tablespoons chopped coriander (cilantro) leaves

RED CURRY WITH DUCK AND LYCHEES

3 tablespoons coconut cream

2 tablespoons red curry paste (page 31)

$^1/_2$ Chinese roast duck, boned and chopped

435 ml (15$^1/_4$ fl oz/ 1$^3/_4$ cups) coconut milk

2 tablespoons fish sauce

1 tablespoon palm sugar (jaggery), or soft brown sugar

225 g (8 oz) tin lychees, drained

110 g (3$^3/_4$ oz) baby tomatoes

7 kaffir lime (makrut) leaves, torn in half

1 handful Thai basil leaves

1 long red chilli, seeded, thinly sliced

In Thailand, this specialty dish is often served during the traditional feasting that accompanies celebratory occasions, such as weddings and the New Year. This is a very rich curry, so serve it alongside a salad.

Put the coconut cream in a wok or saucepan and simmer over medium heat for about 5 minutes, or until the cream separates and a layer of oil forms on the surface. Stir the cream if it starts to brown around the edges. Add the curry paste, stir well to combine and cook until fragrant.

Add roasted duck; stir for 5 minutes. Add coconut milk, fish sauce and palm sugar and simmer over medium heat for 5 minutes. Add the lychees and baby tomatoes and cook a further 1–2 minutes. Add kaffir lime leaves, taste, then adjust seasoning if necessary. Spoon into a serving bowl. Sprinkle with basil leaves and sliced chilli.

EASY! 35 MINUTES SERVES 4

GREEN CURRY OF DUCK AND BABY CORN

Serve with steamed jasmine rice. This is a rich and robust curry, with the chillies and Thai basil packing a hot punch.

Heat a large wok over high heat. Add the coconut cream and fry, stirring all the time, until coconut cream begins to look curdled as the oil begins to seep out and separate.

Add the curry paste and cook, stirring regularly to prevent it from sticking, for about 3 minutes. The paste will begin to be very fragrant as each ingredient begins to cook. Season with fish sauce and sugar, and cook for a further 1–2 minutes.

Add the coconut milk, stock, duck and baby corn and bring to the boil. Reduce the heat, simmer for 4–5 minutes and stir in the lime juice. Just before serving, garnish with the kaffir lime leaves, chillies and Thai basil.

REALLY EASY! · 30 MINUTES · SERVES 6-8

500 ml (17 fl oz/2 cups) coconut cream

3–4 tablespoons green curry paste (page 27)

2 tablespoons fish sauce

1½ tablespoons shaved palm sugar (jaggery), or soft brown sugar

250 ml (9 fl oz/1 cup) coconut milk

250 ml (9 fl oz/1 cup) salt-reduced chicken stock

1 Chinese roast duck, chopped into 2 cm (¾ inch) pieces

125 g (4½ oz) baby corn

2 tablespoons lime juice

3 kaffir lime (makrut) leaves, torn

2 long red chillies, sliced

1 large handful Thai basil

FISH & SEAFOOD

Fish and seafood curries should be eaten on the day that they are made, so choose these curries for when you're feeding all your flatmates or having friends round for a meal. Most seafood curries will work well with any type of seafood, so check with your fishmonger to find out what is cheapest on the day.

BOMBAY-STYLE FISH

To give this a touch of fresh herb flavour, garnish with chopped coriander leaves.

Mix together the garlic, chilli, spices, tamarind and 125 ml (4 fl oz/^{1}/$_2$ cup) of the oil. Place the fish fillets in a shallow dish and spoon marinade over them. Turn the fish over, cover and refrigerate for 30 minutes.

Heat remaining oil in a large heavy-based frying pan and add fish in batches. Cook for 1 minute on each side. Return all fish to the pan, then reduce heat to low and add any remaining marinade and the coconut cream. Season with salt and gently cook for 3–5 minutes, or until the fish is cooked through and flakes easily. If sauce is too runny, lift out the fish, simmer the sauce for a few minutes, then pour it over the fish.

REALLY EASY!

20 MINUTES + MARINATING TIME

SERVES 4

2 garlic cloves, crushed

3 small green chillies, seeded, finely chopped

^{1}/$_2$ teaspoon ground turmeric

^{1}/$_2$ teaspoon ground cloves

^{1}/$_2$ teaspoon ground cinnamon

^{1}/$_2$ teaspoon ground cayenne pepper

1 tablespoon tamarind purée

170 ml (5^1/$_2$ fl oz/^{2}/$_3$ cup) oil

800 g (1 lb 12 oz) pomfret, sole or leatherjacket fillets, skinned

310 ml (10^3/$_4$ fl oz/ 1^1/$_4$ cups) coconut cream

1 kg (2 lb 4 oz) firm white fish fillets, such as sea perch

2 tablespoons fish sauce

310 g (11 oz/2 cups) roughly chopped onion

4 garlic cloves, crushed

2 teaspoons finely chopped ginger

2 teaspoons ground turmeric

1 red chilli, seeded, finely chopped

3 tablespoons oil

A good way to add zing to this curry is to serve it with lemon wedges and a sprinkling of coriander (cilantro) leaves. Squeeze lemon over the curry just before eating.

Cut the fish into 4 cm (1¹/₂ inch) cubes. Place fish pieces in a shallow dish and pour over fish sauce.

Place the onion, garlic, ginger, turmeric, chilli and 1 teaspoon salt into a food processor and process until a paste is formed.

Heat the oil in a deep-sided frying pan; carefully add the spicy paste (at this stage it will splutter), stir it into the oil, lower the heat and cook gently for about 10 minutes. If the mixture starts to burn, add a little water. When paste is cooked it should be a golden brown colour and have oil around the edges.

Remove the fish pieces from the fish sauce and add them to the pan, stirring to cover them with the spicy paste. Raise the heat to medium and cook for about 5 minutes until the fish is cooked through, turning it so it cooks evenly. Transfer fish to a warm serving dish. If the remaining sauce is very liquid, reduce it over high heat until it thickens, then spoon it over the fish.

EASY! 45 MINUTES SERVES 6

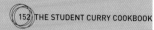

RED CURRY WITH FISH AND BAMBOO SHOOTS

Although there are many styles in the large range of Thai red curries, all have the defining characteristic red colour. Red curries are quite liquid compared to dry curries such as Penang. For this curry be sure to use a firm fish that won't fall apart. A handful of Thai sweet basil leaves and thinly sliced red chilli make a great garnish.

Put the coconut cream in a wok or saucepan and simmer over medium heat for about 5 minutes, or until the cream separates and a layer of oil forms on the surface. Stir the cream if it starts to brown around the edges. Add the curry paste, stir well to combine and cook until fragrant.

Stir in coconut milk, then add the sugar and fish sauce and cook for 2–3 minutes. Add the fish and bamboo shoots and simmer for about 5 minutes, stirring occasionally, until the fish is cooked.

Add the galangal and kaffir lime leaves. Taste, then adjust the seasoning if necessary.

3 tablespoons coconut cream

2 tablespoons red curry paste (page 31)

435 ml (15^{1}/$_{4}$ fl oz/ 1^{3}/$_{4}$ cups) coconut milk

1^{1}/$_{2}$–2 tablespoons shaved palm sugar (jaggery), or soft brown sugar

3 tablespoons fish sauce

350 g (12 oz) skinless firm white fish fillets, cut into 3 cm (1^{1}/$_{4}$ inch) cubes

275 g (9^{3}/$_{4}$ oz) tin bamboo shoots in water, drained, cut into matchsticks

50 g (1^{3}/$_{4}$ oz) galangal, thinly sliced

5 kaffir lime (makrut) leaves, torn in half

REALLY EASY! **30** MINUTES SERVES **4**

FISH BALL CURRY

1 large onion, chopped

1 teaspoon sambal oelek (page 32)

1 tablespoon finely chopped ginger

1 lemongrass stem, white part only, finely chopped

3 tablespoons chopped coriander (cilantro) roots

$1/2$ teaspoon ground cardamom

1 tablespoon tomato paste (concentrated purée)

1 tablespoon oil

1 tablespoon fish sauce

500 ml (17 fl oz/2 cups) coconut milk

750 g (1 lb 10 oz) fish balls (if frozen, thawed)

3 tablespoons chopped coriander (cilantro) leaves

Like many Southeast Asian curries, this one uses lemongrass. When a recipe specifies to use only the white part of the lemongrass, this is because it's the part that is the most tender. The easiest way to find the white part is to peel the outside layers of the lemongrass until you get to the last pink ring.

Place the onion, sambal oelek, ginger, lemongrass, coriander roots, cardamom and tomato paste in a food processor, and process to a smooth paste.

Heat oil in a large saucepan. Add the spice paste and cook, stirring, over medium heat for 4 minutes, or until fragrant.

Stir in 500 ml (17 fl oz/2 cups) water, fish sauce and coconut milk. Bring to the boil, then reduce heat and simmer for 15 minutes, or until the sauce has reduced and thickened slightly.

Add the fish balls and cook for 2 minutes. Don't overcook them or they will become tough and rubbery. Stir in the coriander leaves.

REALLY EASY!   30 MINUTES   SERVES 6

THAI YELLOW CURRY WITH AUBERGINE

Don't feel you have to buy lemon sole for this curry. Some other good choices are cod, hapuka, snapper, kingfish and grouper. Alternatively, if you have a friendly fishmonger, ask for tips about the best (or cheapest) fish of the day.

Heat oil in a large saucepan or wok, then add the curry paste. Cook, stirring often, for 5 minutes, or until fragrant. Pour in the coconut milk, then add the lime leaves, finely grated lime zest and juice, fish sauce, sugar, Thai pea aubergine (if using) and other aubergine. Stir well, bring the mixture to the boil, then reduce the heat to low, cover with a lid and simmer for 15 minutes, or until the curry has thickened slightly and the eggplant is cooked.

Remove the lid from the pan and add bean sprouts, prawns and chunks of fish. Cook for 4–5 minutes, or until the prawns have turned a pale pink and the fish is opaque. Stir in the basil and coriander, add a little salt if you think it needs it, and serve with steamed rice.

Note: Pea aubergines are very small and round, not much bigger than a marble. They are sometimes available at Asian grocery stores.

REALLY EASY! · 45 MINUTES · SERVES 4

3 tablespoons oil

3–4 tablespoons yellow curry paste (page 34)

800 ml (28 fl oz) coconut milk

4 kaffir lime (makrut) leaves (optional)

zest and juice of 1 lime

1 tablespoon fish sauce

1 teaspoon shaved palm sugar (jaggery)

30 Thai pea aubergines (eggplants) (optional)

4 Thai or other baby aubergines (eggplants), quartered or 150 g (5^1/$_2$ oz) regular aubergine

50 g (1^3/$_4$ oz) bean sprouts, trimmed

12 prawns (shrimp), peeled and deveined, tails intact

600 g (1 lb 5 oz) skinless lemon sole fillets, cut into chunks

2 tablespoons Thai basil or other basil leaves

1 tablespoon coriander (cilantro) leaves

TAMARIND FISH CURRY

600 g (1 lb 5 oz) skinless firm white fish fillets

1 teaspoon ground turmeric

pinch powdered saffron

3 garlic cloves, crushed

2 teaspoons lemon juice

1 teaspoon white peppercorns

4 cardamom pods, bruised

1 teaspoon cumin seeds

2 tablespoons coriander seeds

$2^1/2$ tablespoons finely chopped ginger

2 red chillies, thinly sliced

2 tablespoons oil

1 onion, chopped

Continued →

Tamarind is widely used in Indian and Southeast Asian cooking for its sweet–sour flavour and souring properties. Here, the tamarind is balanced by full-bodied peppercorns, cumin and coriander; made aromatic with pungent saffron and sweet cardamom; and creamy with thick yoghurt.

Rinse the fish fillets and pat dry. Prick the fillets with a fork. Combine the turmeric, saffron, garlic, lemon juice and 1 teaspoon of salt then rub over the fish fillets. Refrigerate for 2–3 hours.

Dry-fry the peppercorns, cardamom, cumin and coriander seeds in a frying pan over medium–high heat for 2–3 minutes, or until fragrant. Allow to cool. Using a mortar with a pestle, or spice grinder, crush or grind mixture to a powder and combine with the ginger and chillies.

Heat oil in a heavy-based saucepan over medium heat and add the chopped onion, red and green capsicum, and the ground spice mix. Cook gently for 10 minutes, or until aromatic and the onion is transparent. Increase the heat to high, add diced tomatoes, 250 ml (9 fl oz/1 cup) of water and the tamarind purée. Bring to the boil then reduce to a simmer and cook for 20 minutes.

Rinse paste off the fish and chop into 3 cm (1 inch) pieces. Add to the pan and then continue to simmer for 10 minutes. Stir in the yoghurt and chopped coriander and serve.

1 red and 1 green capsicum (pepper), cut into 2 cm ($^3/_4$ inch) squares

4 Roma (plum) tomatoes, diced

2 tablespoons tamarind purée

185 g (6$^1/_2$ oz/$^3/_4$ cup) plain yoghurt

2 tablespoons chopped coriander (cilantro) leaves

 EASY!

 55 MINUTES + CHILLING TIME SERVES 4

FISH AND PEANUT CURRY

4 tablespoons sesame seeds

1/2 teaspoon cayenne pepper

1/4 teaspoon ground turmeric

1 tablespoon desiccated coconut

2 teaspoons ground coriander

1/2 teaspoon ground cumin

40 g (1 1/2 oz/1/2 cup) crisp fried onion

5 cm (2 inch) piece ginger, chopped

2 garlic cloves, chopped

3 tablespoons tamarind purée

1 tablespoon crunchy peanut butter

1 tablespoon roasted peanuts

8 curry leaves, plus extra, to serve

1 kg (2 lb 4 oz) skinless firm white fish fillets, cut into 2 cm (3/4 inch) cubes

1 tablespoon lemon juice

One of the star ingredients in this dish is crisp fried onion, which can be bought from Asian food stores, or easily prepared at home (see note below).

Put sesame seeds in a heavy-based frying pan, over medium heat and stir until golden. Add the cayenne pepper, turmeric, coconut, ground coriander and cumin and stir until aromatic. Set aside to cool.

Put fried onions, ginger, garlic, tamarind, peanut butter, roasted peanuts, 1 teaspoon salt, sesame spice mix and 500 ml (17 fl oz/2 cups) hot water in a food processor. Process until smooth and thick.

Pour the sauce and curry leaves into a heavy-based frying pan. Simmer, covered, for 15 minutes over low heat. Add fish and simmer for 5 minutes until just cooked through. Gently stir in lemon juice. Season to taste and garnish with curry leaves.

Note: To make crisp fried onion at home, very thinly slice 1 onion, and dry on paper towel for 10 minutes. Fill a deep, heavy-based saucepan one-third full of oil and heat to 160°C (315°F), or until a bread cube dropped into it browns in 30 seconds. Fry onion for 1 minute, or until crisp and golden. Drain well, cool and store in an airtight container for up to 2 weeks.

REALLY EASY! — 40 MINUTES — SERVES 6

THAI GREEN CURRY WITH FISH BALLS

A long-time Thai favourite, this dish features fish balls or dumplings rather than pieces of fish (however, slices of fish can also be used). Thai aubergines (eggplants), galangal and tangy kaffir lime leaves add depth to the spicy curry base,

Put fish fillets in a food processor, or in a mortar with a pestle, and process to a smooth paste.

Put the thick coconut cream from the top of the tin in a saucepan, bring to a rapid simmer over medium heat, stirring occasionally, and cook for 5–10 minutes, until mixture 'splits' (oil starts to separate). Add curry paste and cook for 5 minutes, or until fragrant. Add remaining coconut milk and mix well.

Use a spoon or your wet hands to shape fish paste into small balls, about 2 cm (³/₄ inch) across, and drop them into the coconut milk. Add aubergines, fish sauce and sugar and cook for 12–15 minutes, stirring occasionally, or until cooked.

Stir in galangal and kaffir lime leaves. Taste, then adjust seasoning if necessary. Spoon into a serving bowl and sprinkle with extra coconut milk, basil leaves and sliced chilli.

EASY! | 50 MINUTES | SERVES 4

350 g (12 oz) skinless firm white fish fillets, roughly cut into pieces

3 tablespoons coconut cream

2 tablespoons green curry paste (page 27)

440 ml (15¹/₄ fl oz/ 1³/₄ cups) coconut milk (do not shake the tin), plus extra for topping

175 g (6 oz) Thai apple aubergines (eggplants), quartered

175 g (6 oz) Thai pea aubergines (eggplants)

2 tablespoons fish sauce

2 tablespoons shaved palm sugar (jaggery)

60 g (2¹/₄ oz) galangal, thinly sliced

3 kaffir lime (makrut) leaves, torn in half

1 handful holy basil, to serve

¹/₂ long red chilli, seeded, thinly sliced, to serve

FRIED FISH WITH MILD CURRY

2 tablespoons ghee or oil

4 x 125 g (4^1/$_2$ oz) firm white fish fillets

1 onion, finely chopped

1 teaspoon finely chopped garlic

1 teaspoon ground coriander

2 teaspoons ground cumin

^{1}/$_2$ teaspoon ground turmeric

^{1}/$_2$ teaspoon chilli flakes

1 tablespoon tomato paste (concentrated purée)

This is a great option for people who don't like their curries too hot. The emphasis is on flavour rather than heat.

Melt the ghee in a large pan and cook the fish over medium heat for 1 minute on each side. Transfer the fish to a plate.

Add the onion and garlic to the pan and cook until soft and golden. Add the coriander, cumin, turmeric and chilli and stir-fry for 30 seconds.

Add tomato paste and 125 ml (4 fl oz/^{1}/$_2$ cup) water and simmer for 2 minutes. Add the fish and cook for 1 minute on each side.

REALLY EASY!

25 MINUTES

SERVES 4

COCONUT FISH CURRY

This is a fragrant, richly flavoured Thai style curry. It's good garnished with fresh coriander.

Cut across the fillets to make thick slices. Sprinkle with lemon juice and set aside.

Toast the cumin, fennel seeds and coconut in a dry frying pan until lightly golden and aromatic. Grind to a powder in a spice grinder, or if you don't have one, use a mortar and pestle instead.

Grind ginger, chillies, garlic and onion to a paste and add the ground spices, turmeric and tamarind.

Fry the prepared seasoning paste in the butter for about 1½–2 minutes, stirring. Add 375 ml (13 fl oz/ 1½ cups) water and bring to the boil, then simmer for 6 minutes.

Add the fish with half the coriander and simmer gently for about 6 minutes, or until fish is tender. Serve sprinkled with the remaining coriander.

Note: If tamarind concentrate is unavailable, use 1 tablespoon lemon or lime juice instead.

650 g (1 lb 7 oz) thick white fish fillets

2 teaspoons lemon juice

1 teaspoon cumin seeds

½ teaspoon fennel seeds

45 g (1½ oz/½ cup) desiccated coconut

2 cm (¾ inch) piece ginger, chopped

2 dried chillies, soaked for 15 minutes in hot water

2 garlic cloves

1 onion

¾ teaspoon ground turmeric

2 teaspoons tamarind concentrate

40 g (1½ oz) butter

2 tablespoons chopped coriander (cilantro)

EASY! **35** MINUTES SERVES **6-8**

FISH IN YOGHURT CURRY

1 kg (2 lb 4 oz) skinless, firm white fish fillets

3 tablespoons oil

1 onion, chopped

2 tablespoons finely chopped ginger

6 garlic cloves, crushed

1 teaspoon ground cumin

2 teaspoons ground coriander

1/4 teaspoon ground turmeric

1 teaspoon garam masala (page 36)

185 g (6 1/2 oz/3/4 cup) Greek-style yoghurt

4 long green chillies, seeded, finely chopped

The creamy texture of this dish belies the depth of flavour it gets from the cumin, coriander and turmeric. Thick yoghurt is an excellent way to protect the fish during cooking and it also absorbs some of the sting from the chillies. A thin yoghurt is not suitable for this recipe.

Cut each fish fillet into four pieces and thoroughly pat them dry. Heat the oil in a heavy-based frying pan over low heat and fry the onion until softened and lightly browned. Add the ginger, garlic and spices and stir for 2 minutes. Add the yoghurt and green chilli and bring to the boil, then cover and simmer for 10 minutes.

Slide in fish pieces and simmer for 10–12 minutes, or until fish flakes easily and is cooked through. Don't overcook or the fish will give off liquid and the sauce will split. Serve quickly as the fish will continue cooking in its sauce.

REALLY EASY!

45 MINUTES

SERVES 4

MALAY

Ling works really well in this recipe, but other fish that you can use are flake, hake and coley. Suit yourself with the amount of chillies used, depending on your tolerance for heat.

Combine chillies, onion, garlic, lemongrass, ginger and shrimp paste in a small food processor and process until roughly chopped. Add 2 tablespoons of the oil and process until the mixture forms a smooth paste, regularly scraping down the side of the bowl with a spatula.

Heat remaining oil in a wok or deep heavy-based frying pan and add the paste. Cook for 3–4 minutes over low heat, stirring constantly until the mixture is very fragrant. Add the curry powder and stir for another 2 minutes. Add the coconut milk, tamarind, kecap manis and 250 ml (9 fl oz/1 cup) water to the wok. Bring to the boil, stirring occasionally, then reduce the heat and simmer for 10 minutes, or until slightly thickened.

Add fish, tomato and lemon juice. Season to taste. Simmer for 5 minutes, or until fish is just cooked.

3–6 red chillies, roughly chopped

1 onion, chopped

4 garlic cloves, peeled

3 lemongrass stems, white part only, sliced

4 cm (1 1/2 inch) piece ginger, sliced

2 teaspoons shrimp paste

3 tablespoons oil

1 tablespoon fish curry powder

250 ml (9 fl oz/1 cup) coconut milk

1 tablespoon tamarind concentrate

1 tablespoon kecap manis

500 g (1 lb 2 oz) skinless ling fillets, cut into cubes

2 ripe tomatoes, chopped

1 tablespoon lemon juice

EASY! 40 MINUTES SERVES 4

150 ml (5 fl oz) vegetable stock

1 tablespoon yellow curry paste (page 34)

1 tablespoon tamarind purée

1 tablespoon shaved palm sugar (jaggery), or soft brown palm sugar

1 1/2 tablespoons fish sauce

150 g (5 1/2 oz) green beans, trimmed and cut into 4 cm (1 1/2 inch) lengths

140 g (5 oz/1 cup) sliced, tinned bamboo shoots, rinsed and drained

400 ml (14 fl oz) coconut cream

400 g (14 oz) perch fillet, cubed

1 tablespoon lime juice

As the name suggests, this curry has a warm yellow colour from the spices used in the curry paste. This curry is great with some lime wedges and a few coriander leaves sprinkled over the top for extra colour and flavour.

Pour the vegetable stock into a large saucepan and bring to the boil. Add curry paste and cook, stirring, for 3–4 minutes, or until fragrant. Stir in the combined tamarind purée, 1 tablespoon of fish sauce and the palm sugar. Add the beans and the bamboo shoots, and then cook over medium heat for 3–5 minutes, or until beans are almost tender.

Add the coconut cream and bring to the boil, then reduce heat, add fish and simmer for 3–5 minutes, or until the fish is just cooked. Stir in lime juice and remaining fish sauce.

REALLY EASY! 35 MINUTES SERVES 4

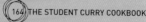

COCONUT PRAWN CURRY

Prawns are the star here, so it makes sense to buy the best quality you can afford. This is a special dish for when you have something to celebrate... great exam results, perhaps?

Peel and devein the prawns, leaving the tails intact. Toss the prawns with the turmeric.

Place onion, garlic, paprika, chilli, cloves, ginger and cardamom in a food processor and process until a paste is formed.

Heat oil in a deep-sided frying pan; carefully add the spicy paste (it will splutter at this stage), stir it into the oil and then cook over low heat for about 10 minutes. If mixture starts to burn, add a little water. When paste is cooked it should be a golden brown colour and will have oil around the edges.

Stir in the prawns, tomatoes and coconut cream, and simmer for about 5 minutes or until the prawns are cooked. Stir in the coriander.

750 g (1 lb 10 oz) raw prawns (shrimp)

1 teaspoon ground turmeric

155 g (5¹/₂ oz/1 cup) roughly chopped onion

4 garlic cloves, crushed

¹/₂ teaspoon paprika

1 teaspoon seeded, finely chopped red chilli

pinch ground cloves

1 teaspoon finely chopped ginger

¹/₄ teaspoon ground cardamom

3 tablespoons oil

2 tomatoes, diced

250 ml (9 fl oz/1 cup) coconut cream

2 tablespoons coriander (cilantro) leaves

EASY!   40 MINUTES   SERVES 4

FIERY PRAWN CURRY

SPICE PASTE

- 6 small dried red chillies
- 1 teaspoon shrimp paste
- 1 teaspoon coriander seeds
- 1 large red onion, roughly chopped
- 6 garlic cloves
- 4cm (1 1/2 inch) piece galangal, roughly chopped
- 4 small red chillies, roughly chopped
- 2 green chillies, roughly chopped
- 41 lemongrass stem, white part only, sliced
- 6 candlenuts (see Note)
- 1/2 teaspoon ground turmeric
- 1 tablespoon oil

Continued →

When using prawns, the most important thing to do is to remove the dark intestinal tract from the back of each one. Start by peeling the prawns from the head end, then make a small slit in the back and pull out the intestinal tract. Some recipes stipulate leaving the tail on — it looks attractive and makes an easy handle to hold the prawn.

Begin by making the spice paste. Soak the dried chillies in hot water until soft, then drain. Wrap the piece of shrimp paste in foil and then grill (broil) for 1–2 minutes under medium heat. Dry-fry the coriander seeds in a small pan until aromatic. Place onion, garlic and drained dried red chillies in a food processor and process until just combined. Add the shrimp paste, coriander seeds, galangal, red and green chilli and lemongrass and process until well combined, scraping down the sides of the bowl with a spatula. Add the candlenuts, turmeric and oil and process until a smooth paste is formed.

Peel and devein the prawns, leaving tails intact. Cut the pineapple into bite-sized pieces and the potatoes into slightly larger pieces.

Place potato in a large pan with enough water to cover and cook for 5 minutes, or until tender. Drain and set aside.

Heat oil in a large frying pan or wok; add the spice paste and cook over medium heat for 5 minutes, stirring constantly. Add pineapple, potato, coconut milk and 125 ml (4 fl oz/½ cup) water and then bring to the boil. Reduce the heat, add the prawns and simmer for 5 minutes. Add the tamarind, sugar and 1 teaspoon salt. Serve with plenty of steamed rice.

Note: Do not eat candlenuts unless they have been cooked first. They are mildly toxic in their raw state.

500 g (1 lb 2 oz) raw prawns (shrimp)

250 g (9 oz) pineapple

250 g (9 oz) potatoes

1 tablespoon oil

250 ml (9 fl oz/1 cup) coconut milk

2 tablespoons tamarind concentrate

1 teaspoon sugar

EASY! 1 HOUR SERVES 4

PRAWNS WITH THAI BASIL

SPICE PASTE

2 dried long red chillies

2 lemongrass stems, white part only, thinly sliced

2.5 cm (1 inch) piece galangal, thinly sliced

5 garlic cloves, crushed

4 red Asian shallots, finely chopped

6 coriander (cilantro) roots, finely chopped

1 teaspoon shrimp paste

1 teaspoon ground cumin

3 tablespoons unsalted peanuts, chopped

600 g (1 lb 5 oz), raw prawns (shrimp), peeled and deveined, tails intact

2 tablespoons oil

185 ml (6 fl oz/¾ cup) coconut milk

2 teaspoons fish sauce

2 teaspoons shaved palm sugar (jaggery)

1 handful Thai basil leaves, to serve

The prawns in this recipe look very attractive because they are butterflied, which means that they are split along the back so they open out.

To make the spice paste, soak chillies in boiling water for 5 minutes, or until soft. Remove seeds and stems and chop. Put chillies and the remaining curry paste ingredients in a food processor, or in a mortar with a pestle, and process or pound to a smooth paste.

Cut each prawn along the back so it opens like a butterfly (leave each prawn joined along the base and at the tail).

Heat the oil in a saucepan or wok and then stir-fry 2 tablespoons of curry paste over a medium heat for 2 minutes, or until fragrant.

Add coconut milk, fish sauce and palm sugar and cook for a few seconds. Add prawns and cook for a few minutes or until cooked through. Taste, then adjust the seasoning if necessary. Serve garnished with Thai basil.

EASY! | **35** MINUTES | SERVES **4**

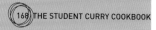

THAI PRAWN AND PUMPKIN CURRY

Flavoured with red curry paste, perfumed by kaffir lime leaves, and seasoned with tamarind, fish sauce, lime juice and chillies, this is a delicious curry with a bit of bite and a lovely tangy taste.

Peel pumpkin and chop into 2 cm ($^3/_4$ inch) cubes. Peel and cut the cucumber in half lengthways, then scrape out seeds with a teaspoon and thinly slice.

Put the thick coconut cream from the top of the tin in a saucepan, bring to a rapid simmer over medium heat, stirring occasionally, and cook for 5–10 minutes, or until mixture 'splits' (the oil starts to separate). Add paste and stir for 2–3 minutes, or until fragrant. Add fish sauce and palm sugar and stir until dissolved.

Add the remaining coconut cream, pumpkin and 3 tablespoons of water, cover and bring to the boil. Reduce to a simmer and cook for 10 minutes, or until pumpkin starts to become tender. Add straw mushrooms, prawns, cucumber, tamarind, chilli, lime juice, kaffir leaves and the coriander roots. Cover, increase the heat and bring to the boil again, then reduce to a simmer and cook for 3–5 minutes, or until prawns are just cooked through. Garnish with bean sprouts and coriander leaves.

EASY! **50** MINUTES SERVES **4**

250 g (9 oz) jap pumpkin (kent squash)

1 Lebanese (short) cucumber

400 ml (13$^1/_2$ fl oz/ 1$^2/_3$ cups) coconut cream (do not shake the tin)

1$^1/_2$ tablespoons red curry paste (page 31)

3 tablespoons fish sauce

2 tablespoons shaved palm sugar (jaggery)

400 g (14 oz) tinned straw mushrooms, drained

500 g (1 lb 2 oz) raw prawns (shrimp), peeled and deveined, tails intact

2 tablespoons tamarind purée

2 red chillies, chopped

1 tablespoon lime juice

4 kaffir lime (makrut) leaves

4 coriander (cilantro) roots, chopped

1 small handful bean sprouts, to serve

1 small handful coriander (cilantro) leaves, to serve

INDIAN-STYLE BUTTER PRAWNS

1 kg (2 lb 4 oz) large raw prawns (shrimp)

100 g (3½ oz) butter

2 large garlic cloves, crushed

1 teaspoon ground cumin

1 teaspoon paprika

1½ teaspoons garam masala (page 36)

2 tablespoons tandoori paste

2 tablespoons tomato paste (concentrated purée)

300 ml (10½ fl oz) thick (double/heavy) cream

1 teaspoon sugar

4 tablespoons plain yoghurt

2 tablespoons chopped coriander (cilantro) leaves

1 tablespoon flaked almonds, toasted

This dish is very rich so serve it with something that will cut through the richness. A fresh salad, steamed vegetables or lemon wedges work well.

Peel and devein the prawns, leaving the tails intact.

Melt butter in a large saucepan over medium heat, then add the garlic, cumin, paprika and 1 teaspoon of the garam masala and cook for 1 minute, or until fragrant. Add the tandoori paste and tomato paste, and cook for a further 2 minutes. Stir in the cream and the sugar, then reduce the heat and simmer for 10 minutes, or until the sauce thickens slightly.

Add the prawns to pan and cook for 8–10 minutes, or until pink and cooked through. Remove the pan from the heat and stir in the yoghurt, the remaining garam masala and half the coriander. Season.

Garnish with the flaked almonds and remaining coriander before serving.

EASY! 35 MINUTES SERVES 4

THAI-STYLE SEAFOOD CURRY WITH TOFU

500 g (1 lb 2 oz) firm white fish

2 tablespoons oil

250 g (9 oz) raw prawns (shrimp), peeled and deveined, tails intact

2 x 400 ml (14oz) tins coconut milk

1 tablespoon red curry paste (page 31)

4 fresh or 8 dried kaffir lime (makrut) leaves

2 tablespoons fish sauce

2 tablespoons finely chopped lemongrass, white part only

2 garlic cloves, crushed

1 tablespoon finely chopped galangal

1 tablespoon shaved palm sugar (jaggery), or soft brown sugar

300 g (10½ oz) silken firm tofu, cut into 1.5 cm (½ inch) cubes

3 tablespoons tinned bamboo shoots, julienned

1 large red chilli

2 teaspoons lime juice

This is a curry bursting with great flavours and textures — definitely one to impress. It's a good one to make when you've got friends coming round because it doesn't keep very well. You can use any kind of firm white fish. Garnish with sliced spring onions and chopped coriander.

Cut fish into 2 cm (³/₄ inch) cubes. Heat the oil in a large frying pan or wok. Sear the fish and prawns over medium heat for 1 minute on each side. Remove from the pan.

Put 3 tablespoons of the coconut milk and the curry paste in a pan and then cook over medium heat for 2 minutes, or until fragrant and the oil separates. Add the remaining coconut milk, lime leaves, fish sauce, lemongrass, garlic, galangal, 1 teaspoon salt and palm sugar. Cook over low heat for 15 minutes.

Add the tofu, bamboo shoots and thinly sliced chilli. Simmer for 3–5 minutes. Return to medium heat, add the seafood and lime juice and cook for 3 minutes, or until the seafood is just cooked. Remove from heat.

EASY! | **50** MINUTES | SERVES **4**

PRAWN AND PINEAPPLE CURRY

The juicy sweetness of this curry comes from the pineapple, while the sourness comes from the unmistakeable flavour of tamarind.

Make the spice paste by putting all of the paste ingredients in a pestle and mortar and pounding them to a paste. Alternatively, you can use a food processor and add 2 tablespoons water. Blend until well combined.

Heat the oil in a wok or saucepan. Add the spice paste and fry until fragrant. Stir in the coconut milk and cook for 2 minutes. Add the pineapple wedges, tamarind purée and kaffir lime leaves and simmer for 5 minutes, or until pineapple begins to soften.

Add the prawns and stir well to cover them in the sauce. Simmer for 5–6 minutes until the prawns are cooked through. Stir in the fish sauce and sugar before serving.

REALLY EASY! · 25 MINUTES · SERVES 4

SPICE PASTE

4 bird's eye chillies, seeded

6 Asian shallots

2 lemongrass stems, white part only, finely chopped

$1/2$ teaspoon shrimp paste

$1/2$ teaspoon ground turmeric

2 tablespoons oil

185 ml (6 fl oz/$3/4$ cup) coconut milk

300 g (10$1/2$ oz) pineapple, cut into small wedges

2 tablespoons tamarind purée

3 kaffir lime (makrut) leaves

250 g (9 oz) raw prawns (shrimp), peeled and deveined

2 teaspoons fish sauce

1 tablespoon palm sugar (jaggery), or soft brown sugar

SOUTHERN INDIAN SEAFOOD CURRY

2 tablespoons oil

^{1}/$_2$ teaspoon fenugreek seeds

10 curry leaves

2 green chillies, split lengthways

1 red onion, sliced

1 tablespoon tamarind concentrate

^{1}/$_2$ teaspoon ground turmeric

^{1}/$_2$ teaspoon paprika

375 ml (13 fl oz/1^1/$_2$ cups) coconut milk

750 g (1 lb 10 oz) mixed seafood

400 g (14 oz) tinned chopped tomatoes

You can change this recipe every time you make it and choose a different selection of seafood depending on what's available, and your budget. You can use any firm white fish fillets, cut into pieces; prawns (shrimp), peeled, deveined and tails intact; scallops and squid, sliced into rings.

Heat oil in a saucepan, add the fenugreek seeds and cook over medium heat until they pop. Add the curry leaves, chillies and onion and cook for about 8 minutes, or until the onion is soft.

Add the tamarind, turmeric, paprika,^{1}/$_2$ teaspoon salt, ^{1}/$_2$ teaspoon ground black pepper and half the coconut milk. Bring to the boil, reduce the heat to a simmer and add the seafood. Cook for 8 minutes, or until it changes colour, turning the seafood during cooking.

Add the tomatoes and the remaining coconut milk. Cover and cook for a further 4 minutes, or until the seafood is tender.

REALLY EASY! 35 MINUTES SERVES 4

LIGHT RED SEAFOOD CURRY

Palm sugar is an important ingredient in many Southeast Asian recipes. It is usually sold in a solid block and needs to be shaved or grated before it can be used. To shave, use a vegetable peeler or the cheese slice option on a cheese grater. If you'd like smaller pieces, shave it with the rough side of a cheese grater.

Remove 250 ml (9 fl oz/1 cup) thick coconut cream from top of the cans (reserve the rest) and place in a wok. Heat until just boiling, then stir in the curry paste. Reduce the heat. Simmer for 10 minutes, or until fragrant and the oil begins to separate.

Stir in the seafood and remaining coconut cream and cook for 5 minutes. Add fish sauce, sugar, lime leaves and chilli, if using, and cook for 1 minute. Stir in half the basil and use the rest to garnish.

2 x 270 ml (9$^{1}/_{2}$ fl oz) tins coconut cream

3 tablespoons chu chee curry paste (page 26)

500 g (1 lb 2 oz) raw king prawns (shrimp), peeled and deveined, tails intact

500 g (1 lb 2 oz) scallops, without roe

2–3 tablespoons fish sauce

2–3 tablespoons shaved palm sugar (jaggery), or soft brown sugar

8 kaffir lime (makrut) leaves, finely shredded

2 small red chillies, thinly sliced, optional

30 g (1 oz/1 cup) Thai basil leaves

THAI JUNGLE CURRY WITH PRAWNS

SPICE PASTE

10–12 dried red chillies

4 red Asian shallots, chopped

4 garlic cloves, sliced

1 lemongrass stem, white part only, sliced

1 tablespoon finely chopped galangal

2 small coriander (cilantro) roots, chopped

1 tablespoon finely chopped ginger

1 tablespoon shrimp paste, dry-roasted

3 tablespoons oil

Continued →

This very hot and spicy curry originated in the city of Chiang Mai in Thailand. Fresh prawns can be expensive, but they are perfect for a special occasion. The recipe is easily adapted if you are on a tight budget. You can substitute chicken or pork for the prawns, or use lean red meat.

To make the spice paste, soak chillies in 250 ml (9 fl oz/1 cup) boiling water for 10 minutes, then drain and place in a food processor with the rest of the curry paste ingredients. Season with salt and white pepper, and process to a smooth paste.

Heat a wok over medium heat, add the oil and stir to coat the side. Add 3 tablespoons of curry paste and the garlic and cook, stirring constantly, for 5 minutes, or until fragrant. Stir in the candlenuts, fish sauce, stock, whisky, prawns, vegetables and lime leaves, and bring to the boil. Reduce the heat and simmer for 5 minutes, or until the prawns and vegetables are cooked through.

Note: Candlenuts are not to be eaten raw as they are mildly toxic when uncooked.

EASY! · 40 MINUTES · SERVES 4

1 tablespoon oil

1 garlic clove, crushed

3 tablespoons ground candlenuts

1 tablespoon fish sauce

300 ml (10^1/$_2$ fl oz) fish stock

1 tablespoon whisky

600 g (1 lb 5 oz) raw prawns (shrimp), peeled and deveined, tails intact

1 small carrot, slivered

200 g (7 oz) snake (yard-long) beans, cut into 2 cm (^{3}/$_4$ inch) lengths

50 g (1^3/$_4$ oz) tinned bamboo shoots, drained

3 kaffir lime (makrut) leaves, crushed

VEGETARIAN

VEGETABLE-BASED DISHES

A wide assortment of vegetables can be used in curries. The general rule with vegetable curries is that hard vegetables, such as root vegetables, should be added first and other more tender vegetables added towards the end of the cooking time. When cooking for a vegetarian, check any curry pastes to ensure they don't contain shrimp paste.

RED LENTIL CURRY

Lentils contain high levels of protein and dietry fibre and are one of the best vegetable sources of iron. This curry is packed with flavour and is good for you, too.

Place lentils, stock and turmeric in a large heavy-based pan. Bring to the boil, reduce the heat and then simmer, covered, for 10 minutes, or until just tender. Stir occasionally and check the mixture is not catching on the bottom of the pan.

Meanwhile, heat the ghee in a small frying pan and add the onion. Cook until soft and golden and add the garlic, chilli, cumin and coriander. Cook, stirring, for 2–3 minutes until fragrant. Stir onions and spices into the lentil mixture and then add the tomato. Simmer over very low heat for 5 minutes, stirring frequently.

Season to taste with salt and pepper, and stir in the coconut milk until heated through.

250 g (9 oz/1 cup) red lentils, rinsed and drained

500 ml (17 fl oz/2 cups) vegetable stock

1/2 teaspoon ground turmeric

50 g (1³/₄ oz) ghee

1 onion, chopped

2 garlic cloves, finely chopped

1 large green chilli, seeded, finely chopped

2 teaspoons ground cumin

2 teaspoons ground coriander

2 tomatoes, chopped

125 ml (4 fl oz/¹/₂ cup) coconut milk

REALLY EASY!   45 MINUTES   SERVES 4

AVIAL

1/2 teaspoon ground turmeric

200 g (7 oz) carrots, cut into batons

200 g (7 oz) orange sweet potato, cut into batons

200 g (7 oz) green beans, trimmed and halved

50 g (1 3/4 oz) grated coconut

5 cm (2 inch) piece ginger, grated

3 green chillies, finely chopped

1 1/2 teaspoons ground cumin

420 ml (14 1/2 fl oz/ 1 2/3 cups) thick plain yoghurt

1 tablespoon oil

10 curry leaves

This dish originated in southern India, and is traditionally served at celebratory banquets and feasts. It is a mixture of vegetables, yoghurt and coconut and is satisfying whether eaten with or without rice.

Bring 500 ml (17 fl oz/2 cups) water to the boil in a saucepan, add turmeric and carrot, reduce the heat and simmer for 5 minutes. Add sweet potato and beans, return to the boil, then reduce heat and simmer for 5 minutes, or until vegetables are almost cooked.

Put the coconut, ginger and chilli in a blender or mortar and pestle, with a little water, and blend or grind to a paste. Add to the vegetables with the cumin and salt and simmer for 2 minutes. Stir in the yoghurt and heat through.

For the final seasoning, heat oil over low heat in a small saucepan. Add curry leaves and allow to crisp. Pour the hot mixture over the vegetables.

EASY! · 30 MINUTES · SERVES 4 · V

To make this recipe suitable for vegetarians, make sure you use a red curry paste that doesn't contain shrimp paste. If you are making the one that's in the Basics chapter (page 31), simply omit the shrimp paste from the recipe.

Heat the oil in a large wok or frying pan. Cook the onion and curry paste for 4 minutes over medium heat, stirring.

Add coconut milk and 250 ml (9 fl oz/1 cup) water, bring to the boil and then simmer, uncovered, for 5 minutes. Add the potato, cauliflower and kaffir lime leaves, and simmer for 7 minutes. Add snake beans, red capsicum, corn and peppercorns and cook for 5 minutes or until vegetables are tender.

Stir in the basil, soy sauce, lime juice and sugar.

1 tablespoon oil

1 onion, chopped

1–2 tablespoons red curry paste (without shrimp paste) (page 31)

375 ml (13 fl oz/1 1/2 cups) coconut milk

2 potatoes, chopped

200 g (7 oz) cauliflower florets

6 kaffir lime (makrut) leaves

150 g (5 1/2 oz) snake (yard-long) beans, cut into 3 cm (1 1/4 inch) pieces

1/2 red capsicum (pepper), cut into strips

10 fresh baby corn spears, halved lengthways

1 tablespoon green peppercorns, roughly chopped

1 handful Thai basil, finely chopped

2 tablespoons soy sauce

1 tablespoon lime juice

2 teaspoons soft brown sugar

CAULIFLOWER, PEA AND TOMATO CURRY

1 small cauliflower, separated into small florets

235 g (8 1/2 oz/1 1/2 cups) fresh or frozen green peas

1 onion, thinly sliced

1 teaspoon crushed garlic

1 teaspoon grated ginger

4 tablespoons ghee

3/4 teaspoon ground tumeric

1 tablespoon ground coriander

1 tablespoon vindaloo paste (page 33)

2 teaspoons sugar

2 cardamom pods, split

185 g (6 1/2 oz/3/4 cup) plain yoghurt

2 large tomatoes, cut into thin wedges

You can serve this as a side dish for 6 people or as a main dish for 3 or 4. It is very simple and has a pleasing mix of textures and flavours.

Boil the cauliflower and peas in water until tender. Drain and set aside.

Cook the onion, garlic and ginger in the ghee until golden and tender. Add the turmeric, coriander, vindaloo paste, sugar, cardamom and yoghurt and then cook for 3–4 minutes. Add tomatoes and cook for a further 3–4 minutes.

Add cauliflower and peas. Simmer for 3–4 minutes

REALLY EASY! 45 MINUTES SERVES 4-6 V

MUSAMAN VEGETABLE CURRY

This recipe is a good one to try if you are new to curry making. It's sumptuously spiced and well seasoned, but not fiery or overly rich. And, it has a lightness of flavour not seen in many curries. If you are serving this dish for vegetarians, omit the shrimp paste from the curry paste or choose a variety without shrimp paste.

Heat oil in a large saucepan, add curry paste and cook, stirring, over medium heat for 2 minutes, or until fragrant. Add the vegetables, cinnamon stick, kaffir lime leaf, bay leaf and enough water to cover (about 500 ml/17 fl oz/2 cups), and then bring to the boil. Reduce the heat and simmer, covered, stirring frequently, for 30–35 minutes, or until the vegetables are cooked.

Stir in the coconut cream and cook, uncovered, for 4 minutes, stirring frequently, until thickened slightly. Stir in the lime juice, palm sugar and chopped basil. Add a little water if the sauce is too dry. Top with the peanuts and basil leaves.

REALLY EASY! · 1 HOUR · SERVES 4-6 · V

1 tablespoon oil

3 tablespoons musaman curry paste (without shrimp paste) (page 29)

250 g (9 oz) baby onions

500 g (1 lb 2 oz) baby new potatoes

300 g (10¹/₂ oz) carrots, cut into 3 cm (1¹/₄ inch) pieces

225 g (8 oz) tinned whole baby button mushrooms (champignons), drained

1 cinnamon stick

1 kaffir lime (makrut) leaf

1 bay leaf

250 ml (9 fl oz/1 cup) coconut cream

1 tablespoon lime juice

3 teaspoons shaved palm sugar (jaggery), or soft brown sugar

1 tablespoon finely chopped Thai basil, plus extra to serve

1 tablespoon crushed toasted peanuts

COCONUT VEGETABLE CURRY

2 tablespoons oil

1 large red onion, roughly chopped

3 garlic cloves, finel chopped

4 red chillies, finely chopped

2 bay leaves, torn

250 ml (9 fl oz/1 cup) coconut milk

1 tablespoon tamarind concentrate

2 teaspoons sugar

500 g (1 lb 2 oz) combined chopped pumpkin (winter squash), potato and carrot

125 g (4½ oz) chopped green beans

125 g (4½ oz) chopped courgette (zucchini)

2 large tomatoes, peeled and roughly chopped

150 g (5½ oz) baby spinach leaves

2 tablespoons desiccated coconut

2 tablespoons lemon juice

Other root vegetables, while not as authentic, could be used in this recipe. For example, try replacing the carrots with parsnips, swedes or turnips.

Heat oil in a large heavy-based pan; add onion, garlic and chilli, and then cook over medium heat for 5 minutes, stirring regularly. Add the bay leaves, coconut milk, tamarind, sugar and ¼ teaspoon salt Bring to the boil, then reduce the heat and simmer, uncovered, for 5 minutes.

Add pumpkin, potato and carrot. Cover and cook for 7 minutes, stirring occasionally. Add beans and courgette and cook for another 5 minutes, or until the vegetables are tender. Stir in the tomato and spinach and cook, uncovered, for 2 minutes. If the curry is thicker than you like, add a little water.

Just before serving, remove the bay leaves, stir in the coconut and sprinkle with lemon juice.

REALLY EASY! — 1 HOUR — SERVES 4 — ✓

THAI YELLOW VEGETABLE CURRY

Yellow curries are from Thailand's southern areas and are characterised by the use of spices such as coriander, cumin and turmeric in the paste.

Heat oil in a large saucepan, add the onion and cook over medium heat for 4–5 minutes, or until softened and just turning golden. Add the yellow curry paste and cook, stirring, for 2 minutes, or until fragrant.

Add all the vegetables and cook, stirring, over high heat for 2 minutes. Pour in the vegetable stock, reduce the heat to medium and cook, covered, for 15–20 minutes, or until the vegetables are tender. Cook, uncovered, over high heat for 5–10 minutes, or until the sauce has reduced slightly.

Stir in the coconut cream and season with salt to taste. Bring to the boil, stirring frequently, then reduce the heat and simmer for 5 minutes.

3 tablespoons oil

1 onion, finely chopped

2 tablespoons yellow curry paste (page 34)

200 g (7 oz) all-purpose potatoes, diced

200 g (7 oz) courgette (zucchini), diced

150 g (5¹/₂ oz) red capsicum (pepper), diced

100 g (3¹/₂ oz) beans, trimmed and halved

50 g (1³/₄ oz) tinned bamboo shoots, sliced

250 ml (9 fl oz/1 cup) vegetable stock

400 ml (14 fl oz) coconut cream

EASY! · 1 HOUR · SERVES 6 · V

GREEN CURRY WITH SWEET POTATO

1 tablespoon oil

1 onion, chopped

1–2 tablespoons green curry paste (without shrimp paste) (page 27)

1 (aubergine) eggplant, quartered and sliced

400 ml (14 fl oz) tin coconut milk

250 ml (9 fl oz/1 cup) vegetable stock

6 kaffir lime (makrut) leaves

1 orange sweet potato, cut into cubes

2 teaspoons soft brown sugar

2 tablespoons lime juice

2 teaspoons lime zest

Traditionally, green curry paste contains shrimp paste, so be careful to choose a commercial green curry paste that doesn't contain any shrimp. Alternatively, you can make the green curry paste from the Basics chapter (page 27) and simply omit the shrimp paste from the recipe.

Heat oil in a large wok or frying pan. Add the onion and curry paste and cook, stirring, over medium heat for 3 minutes. Add the eggplant and cook for a further 4–5 minutes, or until softened. Pour in the coconut milk and stock, bring to the boil, then reduce the heat and simmer for 5 minutes. Add the lime leaves and sweet potato and cook, stirring occasionally, for 10 minutes, or until the vegetables are very tender.

Mix in the sugar, lime juice and lime zest until they are well combined with the vegetables. Season to taste with salt.

REALLY EASY! · 40 MINUTES · SERVES 4-6

DHAL WITH VEGETABLES

In India, dahl refers to both the dried pulse and the finished dish. Lentils are used in this recipe, but chickpeas and other beans and peas would be good substitutes.

Rinse the lentils, separately, under cold water until the water runs clear, then drain well. Put the yellow lentils in a small bowl, cover with water and stand for 30 minutes, then drain well.

Heat ghee in a saucepan over medium heat. Cook the onion and garlic, stirring, for about 3 minutes, or until the onion is soft.

Stir in the spices and cook, stirring, for 30 seconds, or until fragrant. Add lentils, tomatoes and stock. Bring to the boil over high heat, then reduce the heat to low and simmer, covered, for 20 minutes.

Add in the carrots and cauliflower and stir well. Cover and cook for 10 minutes. Add the beans and cook, covered, for a further 5 minutes, or until the lentils are tender and the vegetables are cooked. Season to taste. Stir in the cream.

150 g (5^{1}/2 oz/scant ^{2}/3 cup) yellow lentils

150 g (5^{1}/2 oz/^{2}/3 cup) red lentils

1 tablespoon ghee

1 onion, chopped

2 garlic cloves, crushed

1 tablespoon fenugreek seeds

2 teaspoons ground cumin

2 teaspoons ground coriander

^{1}/2 teaspoon ground turmeric

400 g (14 oz) tin chopped tomatoes

750 ml (26 fl oz/3 cups) vegetable stock

2 carrots, chopped

250 g (9 oz) cauliflower florets

150 g (5^{1}/2 oz) green beans, trimmed and halved

3 tablespoons thick (double/heavy) cream

EASY! · 45 MINUTES + STANDING TIME · SERVES 6 · V

PUMPKIN, GREEN BEAN AND CASHEW CURRY

500 ml (17 fl oz/2 cups) coconut cream (do not shake the tin)

3 teaspoons yellow curry paste (page 34)

125 ml (4 fl oz/½ cup) vegetable or chicken stock

500 g (1 lb 2 oz) jap pumpkin (kent squash), peeled and diced

300 g (10½ oz) green beans, trimmed and halved

2 tablespoons soy sauce

2 tablespoons lime juice

1 tablespoon shaved palm sugar (jaggery), or soft brown sugar

1 handful coriander (cilantro) leaves

3 tablespoons cashew nuts, toasted

Store nuts in the refrigerator. The oil in them can turn rancid if they are kept in a warm place. Ideally, buy nuts in small quantities, as needed.

Spoon the thick coconut cream from the top of the tin into the wok, and heat until boiling. Add the curry paste, then reduce heat and simmer, stirring, for 5 minutes, until the oil begins to separate.

Add remaining coconut cream, stock and pumpkin, and simmer for 10 minutes. Add green beans and cook for a further 8 minutes, or until the vegetables are tender.

Stir in soy sauce, lime juice, and palm sugar gently. Sprinkle with coriander leaves and cashew nuts.

REALLY EASY! • 35 MINUTES • SERVES 4 • V

DUM ALOO

Make the spice paste by lightly crushing cardamom pods with the flat side of a heavy knife. Remove the seeds, discarding the pods. Put seeds and the rest of the spice paste ingredients in a food processor, or in a mortar with a pestle, and then process or pound to a smooth paste.

Bring a large saucepan of salted water to the boil. Add potato, cook for 5–6 minutes, or until tender, then drain.

Put onions in food processor and process in short bursts until finely chopped but not until reduced to a purée. Heat oil in a large pan, add onion and cook over low heat for 5 minutes. Add the spice paste and cook, stirring, for 5 minutes, or until fragrant. Stir in potato, turmeric, salt and 250 ml (9 fl oz/ 1 cup) water.

Reduce the heat and then simmer, tightly covered, for 10 minutes, or until the potato is cooked but not breaking up and the sauce has thickened slightly.

Combine besan with yoghurt, add to potato mixture and cook, stirring, over low heat for 5 minutes, or until thickened. Garnish with coriander leaves

SPICE PASTE

4 cardamom pods

1 teaspoon grated ginger

2 garlic cloves, crushed

3 red chillies

1 teaspoon cumin seeds

3 tablespoons cashew nuts

1 tablespoon white poppy seeds

1 cinnamon stick

6 cloves

---

1 kg (2 lb 4 oz) all-purpose potatoes, cubed

2 onions, roughly chopped

2 tablespoons oil

$1/2$ teaspoon ground turmeric

1 teaspoon besan (chickpea flour)

250 g (9 oz/1 cup) plain yoghurt

EASY! · 45 MINUTES · SERVES 6 · V

AUBERGINE COCONUT CURRY

500 g (1 lb 2 oz) slim aubergines (eggplants), trimmed and cut into 3 cm (1¼ inch) chunks

4 tablespoons vegetable oil

1 tablespoon panch phoran (page 38)

2 teaspoons ground cumin

1 teaspoon ground turmeric

1 red onion, finely sliced

3 garlic cloves, chopped

1 long green chilli, seeded, finely chopped

8 dried curry leaves (see Note)

400 ml (14 fl oz) coconut milk

Red onions have a milder, slightly sweet taste compared to other types of onions.

Put the aubergine in a colander and sprinkle with salt. Set aside for 15 minutes to sweat. Rinse, drain and pat dry with paper towel.

Heat 2 tablespoons of oil in a large heavy-based non-stick frying pan. Fry aubergine for 5 minutes, stirring frequently, or until lightly browned. Remove to a side plate.

Heat remaining oil in the frying pan. Add panch phoran, cumin and turmeric and cook for 1 minute, or until aromatic. Add the onion and cook for about 3 minutes, or until onion is cooked.

Stir in the garlic, chilli and curry leaves and add the aubergine. Stir to coat in the spices. Stir in the coconut milk and 250 ml (9 fl oz/1 cup) of water. Season with salt. Cook, stirring frequently, for 20 minutes, or until the eggplant is cooked and the sauce is thick. Serve hot or at room temperature.

Note: Dried curry leaves are available from Asian food stores and some large supermarkets.

REALLY EASY! · 50 MINUTES + RESTING TIME · SERVES 6 · V

Traditonally, chu chee curry paste contains shrimp, so choose a commercial paste without any, or omit the shrimp paste from the recipe in the Basics Chapter (page 26).

Heat the oil in a large saucepan, add the onion and cook over medium heat for 4–5 minutes, or until starting to brown. Add the curry paste and cook, stirring, for 2 minutes.

Stir in the coconut milk and 125 ml (4 fl oz/^{1}/$_{2}$ cup) water; season with salt. Bring slowly to the boil, stirring constantly. Add tofu puffs, then reduce heat and simmer, stirring frequently, for 5 minutes, or until the sauce thickens slightly.

1 tablespoon oil

----

1 onion, finely chopped

----

3 tablespoons chu chee curry paste (without shrimp paste) (page 26)

----

500 ml (17 fl oz/2 cups) coconut milk

----

200 g (7 oz) fried tofu puffs, halved on the diagonal

CHOKO, CASHEW AND COCONUT MILK CURRY

150 g (5¹/₂ oz/1 cup) raw cashew nuts

2 tablespoons oil

1 onion, thinly sliced

2 garlic cloves, crushed

1 cinnamon stick

1 teaspoon ground turmeric

8 curry leaves

400 ml (14 fl oz) coconut milk

4 small chokos (chayotes)

1 small handful Thai basil, chopped

The choko is a fruit that is used as a vegetable. It belongs to the pumpkin family. It has a bland taste and absorbs flavours well. Marrows or courgettes can be used instead.

Soak the cashews in water overnight. Drain and dry on paper towels. Finely chop half of the cashews by hand or in a food processor and reserve. Heat the oil in a saucepan and add the whole cashews. Fry over medium–low heat until golden. Remove with a slotted spooon and reserve.

Add onion and garlic to pan and fry until softened, for about 5 minutes, then add the cinnamon stick, turmeric, and curry leaves. Cook, stirring often, for 2 minutes. Add coconut milk and 350 ml (12 fl oz) water. Bring slowly to the boil and then simmer for 5 minutes.

Peel chokos and cut each into 4 wedges. Discard the seed and slice the flesh into chunks. Add to the pan and return the mixture to a simmer. Stir through the chopped cashews and basil, remove from the heat and allow to rest for 2–3 minutes before serving.

EASY! · 40 MINUTES + SOAKING TIME · SERVES 4 · V

INDONESIAN PUMPKIN AND SPINACH CURRY

This curry contains some of the classic ingredients of Indonesian cooking, including, shallots, galangal candlenuts and sambal oelek. Sambal means hot and spicy, which gives you a good idea of how the finished dish will taste.

To make the spice paste, put all paste ingredients in a food processor, or in a mortar with a pestle, and process or pound to a smooth paste.

Heat oil in a large saucepan, add the curry paste and cook, stirring, over low heat for 3–5 minutes, or until fragrant. Add the onion and cook for a further 5 minutes, or until softened.

Add the pumpkin and half the vegetable stock and cook, covered, for 10 minutes, or until the pumpkin is almost cooked through. Add more stock, if required. Add spinach, coconut cream and sugar, and season with salt. Bring to the boil, stirring constantly, then reduce the heat and simmer for 3–5 minutes, or until the spinach is cooked and the sauce has thickened slightly. Serve immediately.

Note: Candlenuts must be cooked as they are slightly toxic when raw.

SPICE PASTE

3 candlenuts (see Note)

1 tablespoon raw peanuts

3 red Asian shallots, chopped

2 garlic cloves

2–3 teaspoons sambal oelek (page 32)

$1/4$ teaspoon ground turmeric

1 teaspoon grated galangal

2 tablespoons oil

1 onion, finely chopped

600 g (1 lb 5 oz) butternut pumpkin (squash), cut into 2 cm ($3/4$ inch) cubes

125 ml (4 fl oz/$1/2$ cup) vegetable stock (or as required)

350 g (12 oz) English spinach, roughly chopped

400 ml (14 fl oz) coconut cream

$1/4$ teaspoon sugar

1 half-ripe pineapple, cored, cut into chunks

1/2 teaspoon ground turmeric

1 star anise

7 whole cloves

1 cinnamon stick, broken into small pieces

7 cardamom pods, bruised

1 tablespoon oil

1 onion, finely chopped

1 teaspoon grated ginger

1 garlic clove

5 red chillies, chopped

1 tablespoon sugar

3 tablespoons coconut cream

Pineapple adds a touch of tart sweetness to curries and is popular in vegetarian meals. Here, it is mixed with hot chillies, creamy coconut and cloves and cinnamon to create a refreshing dish.

Place the pineapple in a saucepan, cover with water and add the ground turmeric. Wrap the star anise, cloves, cinnamon and cardamom pods in a square of muslin (cheesecloth), and tie securely with string. Add to the pan and cook over medium heat for 10 minutes. Squeeze the bag to extract any flavour, then discard.

Heat the oil in a frying pan, add the onion, ginger, garlic and chilli, and cook, stirring, for 1–2 minutes, or until fragrant. Add pineapple, and the cooking liquid, sugar and salt to taste. Cook for 2 minutes, then stir in the coconut cream. Cook, stirring, over low heat for 3–5 minutes, or until the sauce thickens. Serve hot or cold.

REALLY EASY! | 40 MINUTES | SERVES 6 | V

AROMATIC VEGETABLE AND CHICKPEA CURRY

This recipe is easily adapted to make use of other seasonal root vegetables.

Heat the oil in a saucepan over medium heat. Cook onion and garlic, stirring, for 3 minutes, or until the onion is transparent. Add the cumin, turmeric, coriander and chilli, and stir until the spices are fragrant. Add the potatoes and carrots to pan. Cook for 1 minute, stirring to coat in the spice mix. Stir in the tomatoes, peas, chickpeas and vegetable stock. Cover saucepan with a lid and cook for 20 minutes, stirring occasionally.

Stir in spinach leaves and cook until wilted. Season the curry with salt and pepper to taste.

REALLY EASY! · 35 MINUTES · SERVES 4 · V

1 tablespoon peanut oil

1 onion, chopped

2 garlic cloves, crushed

$1\frac{1}{2}$ teaspoons ground cumin

1 teaspoon ground turmeric

$1\frac{1}{2}$ teaspoons ground coriander

1 green chilli, seeded, chopped

2 all-purpose potatoes, chopped into 4 cm ($1\frac{1}{2}$ inch) pieces

2 carrots, cut into 4 cm ($1\frac{1}{2}$ inch) pieces

400 g (14 oz) tinned chopped tomatoes

80 g ($2\frac{3}{4}$ oz/$\frac{1}{2}$ cup) frozen peas

420 g (15 oz) tinned chickpeas, drained, rinsed

500 ml (17 fl oz/2 cups) vegetable stock

90 g ($3\frac{1}{4}$ oz) baby English spinach leaves

PEA, EGG AND RICOTTA CURRY

4 hard-boiled eggs

$^1/_2$ teaspoon ground turmeric

3 tablespoons ghee or oil

1 bay leaf

2 small onions, finely chopped

1 teaspoon finely chopped garlic

$1^1/_2$ teaspoons ground coriander

$1^1/_2$ teaspoons garam masala (page 36)

$^1/_2$ teaspoon chilli powder, optional

125 g ($4^1/_2$ oz/$^1/_2$ cup) chopped, canned, peeled tomatoes

Continued →

This is a colourful dish, with its golden turmeric-coated eggs and green peas. Baked ricotta gives it a pleasing texture, rather in the way that tofu does to other curry recipes, and it absorbs the flavours of the other ingredients. Baked ricotta does not keep very well so use it within a couple of days of purchase. Store it, covered, in the refrigerator.

Peel the eggs and coat them with the turmeric.

Melt the ghee in a large pan and cook eggs over moderate heat for 2 minutes until light brown; stir constantly. Set aside.

Add bay leaf, onion and garlic to pan and cook over medium–high heat, stirring frequently, until well reduced and pale gold. Lower heat if the mixture is browning too quickly. Add coriander, garam masala and chilli powder, if using, and cook until fragrant.

Add tomato, tomato paste and 125 ml (4 fl oz/½ cup) water; cover and simmer for 5 minutes. Return the eggs to the pan with the ricotta, ¼ teaspoon salt, yoghurt and peas and cook 5 minutes. Discard bay leaf. Sprinkle curry with coriander.

Note: Baked ricotta is available from delicatessens and some supermarkets. To make on your own, preheat oven to 160°C (315°F/Gas 2–3). Slice 500 g (1 lb/2 oz) fresh ricotta (not blended ricotta) into 3 cm (1¼ inch) thick slices. Place on a lightly greased baking tray and bake for 25 minutes.

1 tablespoon tomato paste (concentrated purée)

125 g (4½ oz/½ cup) baked ricotta, cut into 1 cm (½ inch) cubes

1 tablespoon yoghurt

80 g (2¾ oz/½ cup) frozen peas

2 tablespoons finely chopped coriander (cilantro) leaves

REALLY EASY! · 45 MINUTES · SERVES 4 · V

CASHEW NUT CURRY

1 pandanus leaf

750 ml (26 fl oz/3 cups) coconut milk

1 onion, chopped

1 tablespoon grated ginger

1/2 teaspoon ground turmeric

3 cm (1 1/4 inch) piece galangal

2 green chillies, seeded, finely chopped

8 curry leaves

1 cinnamon stick

250 g (9 oz) raw cashew nuts

Pandanus leaves are long and slender in shape, and are used widely in South East Asia for various purposes; in clothing and textiles, handicrafts and decorations, foods, medications and fishing. In Thai cooking, they are used to bring nutty flavours and earthy fragrances to dishes.

Shred the pandanus leaf lengthways into about 3 sections, and tie into a large knot. Combine the coconut milk, onion, ginger, turmeric, galangal, chilli, curry leaves, cinnamon stick and pandanus leaf in a pan and bring to the boil. Reduce the heat and simmer for 20 minutes.

Add cashew nuts, and cook for another 30 minutes, or until the nuts are tender.

Remove the curry from the heat; discard the galangal, cinnamon stick and pandanus leaf.

REALLY EASY! · 1 1/4 HOURS · SERVES 4-6 · V

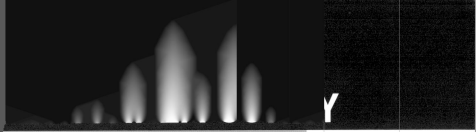

Chickpeas are a good staple. Tinned chickpeas will work in this recipe, too. No soaking is needed.

Place the chickpeas in a bowl, cover with water and leave to soak overnight. Drain, rinse and place in a large saucepan. Cover with plenty of water and bring to the boil, then reduce the heat and simmer for 40 minutes, or until soft. Drain.

Heat oil in a large saucepan, add onion and cook over medium heat for 15 minutes, or until golden brown. Add tomato, ground coriander and cumin, chilli powder, turmeric and channa (chole) masala, and 500 ml (17 fl oz/2 cups) water, and then cook for 10 minutes, or until tomato is soft. Add chickpeas, season well with salt and cook for 7–10 minutes, or until the sauce thickens. Transfer to a serving dish. Place the ghee or butter on top and allow to melt before serving. Garnish with sliced onion, and mint and coriander leaves.

Note: Channa (chole) masala is a spice blend specifically used in this dish. It is available at Indian grocery stores. Garam masala can be used as a substitute if it is unavailable, but this will alter the final flavour.

220 g (7³/₄ oz/1 cup) dried chickpeas

2 tablespoons oil

2 onions, finely chopped

2 large ripe tomatoes, chopped

¹/₂ teaspoon ground coriander

1 teaspoon ground cumin

1 teaspoon chilli powder

¹/₄ teaspoon ground turmeric

1 tablespoon channa (chole) masala (see Note)

20 g (³/₄ oz) ghee or butter

1 small onion, sliced

REALLY EASY! — 45 MINUTES — SERVES 2 — V

THAI RED SQUASH CURRY

2 tablespoons oil

1–2 tablespoons red curry paste (without shrimp paste) (page 31)

400 ml (14 fl oz) coconut milk

2 tablespoons soy sauce

125 ml (4 fl oz/^{1}/$_2$ cup) vegetable stock

2 teaspoons shaved palm sugar (jaggery), or soft brown sugar

700 g (1 lb 9 oz) baby (pattypan) squash, halved, or quartered if large

100 g (3^1/$_2$ oz) baby corn, halved lengthways

100 g (3^1/$_2$ oz) snow peas (mangetout), trimmed

2 teaspoons lime juice

4 tablespoons unsalted toasted cashews, coarsely chopped

Sugar snap peas can be used in place of snow peas, or use a mixture of the two. As red curry paste sometimes contains shrimp, make sure you choose a commercial paste without any, or simply omit the shrimp paste from the recipe in the Basics chapter (page 31)

Heat the oil in a large saucepan over medium–high heat and fry the curry paste for 1–2 minutes, or until the paste separates. Add coconut milk, soy sauce, stock and palm sugar and stir until the sugar has melted. Bring to the boil.

Add squash to pan and return to the boil. Add baby corn and simmer, covered, for 12–15 minutes, or until squash is just tender. Add the snow peas and lime juice and simmer, uncovered, for 1 minute. Serve with the cashews scattered over the top.

Note: If baby squash are unavailable, use courgette (zucchini), cut into slices 2.5 cm (1 inch) thick.

REALLY EASY! 40 MINUTES SERVES 4 V

SRI LANKAN AUBERGINE CURRY

There are many similarities between Indian and Sri Lankan cooking, but it would be wrong to think they are interchangeable. Crucially, their curry powders differ. Sri Lankan curry powder has a more dark and intense flavour.

Mix half the ground turmeric with 1 teaspoon salt and rub into the aubergine, ensuring the cut surfaces are well coated. Put in a colander and leave for 1 hour. Rinse well and put on crumpled paper towel to remove any excess moisture.

Fill a deep heavy-based saucepan one-third full of oil and heat to 180°C (350°F), or until a cube of bread dropped into the oil browns in 15 seconds. Cook the aubergine in batches for 1 minute, or until golden brown. Drain on crumpled paper towel.

Heat the extra oil in a large saucepan, add onion and cook over medium heat for 5 minutes, or until browned. Add curry powder, garlic, curry leaves, chilli powder, aubergine and remaining turmeric to pan, and cook for 2 minutes. Stir in coconut cream and 250 ml (9 fl oz/1 cup) water, and season with salt. Reduce heat and simmer over low heat for 3 minutes, or until aubergine is cooked and sauce has thickened slightly. Garnish with curry leaves.

1 teaspoon ground turmeric

12 slender aubergines (eggplants), cut into 4 cm (1 1/2 inch) rounds

oil, for deep-frying, plus 2 tablespoons, extra

2 onions, finely chopped

2 tablespoons Sri Lankan curry powder (page 39)

2 garlic cloves, crushed

8 curry leaves, roughly chopped, plus extra whole leaves for garnish

1/2 teaspoon chilli powder

250 ml (9 fl oz/1 cup) coconut cream

EASY! · 40 MINUTES + STANDING TIME · SERVES 6 · V

DRY POTATO AND PEA CURRY

750 g (1 lb 10 oz) potatoes

2 teaspoons brown mustard seeds

2 tablespoons ghee or oil

2 onions, sliced

2 garlic cloves, crushed

2 teaspoons grated ginger

1 teaspoon ground turmeric

$1/2$ teaspoon chilli powder

1 teaspoon ground cumin

1 teaspoon garam masala (page 36)

100 g ($3^1/2$ oz/$^2/3$ cup) peas

2 tablespoons chopped mint

This is a wonderfully sustaining dish and is very inexpensive to make. If fresh mint is not available, don't be tempted to use dried. Substitute coriander leaves or parsley.

Peel the potatoes and cut them into small cubes.

Place the mustard seeds in a large dry pan and cook over medium heat until the seeds start to pop. Add the ghee, onion, garlic and ginger, and cook, stirring, until the onion is soft.

Add the turmeric, chilli powder, cumin, garam masala and potato; stir until the potato is coated. Add 125 ml (4 fl oz/$^1/2$ cup) water, cover and simmer for 15–20 minutes, or until the potato is just tender, stirring occasionally.

Stir in the peas and stir until combined; season with salt and pepper to taste. Simmer, covered, for a further 3–5 minutes, or until the potato is cooked through and the liquid is absorbed. Stir in the mint.

REALLY EASY!   40 MINUTES   SERVES 4   V

AUBERGINE CURRY

Aubergine (eggplant) can have a very bitter taste, which the process of salting and rinsing helps to remove. Aubergine absorbs other flavours well and adds a silky soft texture to this dish.

Cut the aubergine into 2 cm ($^3/_4$ inch) cubes and sprinkle with $^1/_2$ teaspoon salt. Set aside for 1 hour. Drain and rinse. Then pat dry with paper towels.

Chop the tomatoes into rough dice. Heat the oil in a heavy-based saucepan over medium heat. Add the fenugreek and fennel seeds. When they start to crackle, add the garlic, onion and curry leaves and cook for 3–5 minutes or until onion is transparent. Add the eggplant and stir for 6 minutes, or until it begins to soften. Add the ground spices, tomatoes, tomato juice, tamarind and sliced fresh chillies.

Bring to the boil, then reduce to a simmer, cover and continue to cook for about 35 minutes, or until aubergine is very soft. Stir in the coconut cream and coriander and season to taste.

REALLY EASY!

55 MINUTES + STANDING TIME

SERVES 4

V

1 large (500 g/1 lb 2 oz) aubergine (eggplant)

2 small tomatoes

2 tablespoons oil

3 teaspoons fenugreek seeds

3 teaspoons fennel seeds

4 garlic cloves, crushed

1 large onion, finely diced

4 curry leaves

1$^1/_2$ tablespoons ground coriander

2 teaspoons ground turmeric

125 ml (4 fl oz/$^1/_2$ cup) tomato juice

2 tablespoons tamarind purée

2 red chillies, finely sliced

125 ml (4 fl oz/$^1/_2$ cup) coconut cream

1 handful coriander (cilantro) leaves, chopped

WHITE VEGETABLE CURRY

300 g (10^1/$_2$ oz) jap pumpkin (kent squash)

200 g (7 oz) all-purpose potato

250 g (9 oz) okra

2 tablespoons oil

1 garlic clove, crushed

3 green chillies, seeded, very finely chopped

^{1}/$_2$ teaspoon ground turmeric

^{1}/$_2$ teaspoon fenugreek seeds

1 onion, chopped

8 curry leaves

1 cinnamon stick

500 ml (17 fl oz/2 cups) coconut milk

Okra is the edible fruit pod of a plant related to the hibiscus. It is a good source of fibre and vitamins. The process of slow cooking it releases a sticky, natural thickener. Choose firm, bright green pods.

Peel the pumpkin and potato and then cut them into 2 cm (^{3}/$_4$ inch) cubes. Trim the okra stems. Ignore any sticky, glutinous liquid that emerges because this will disappear as the okra cooks.

Heat the oil in a large heavy-based pan; add the garlic, chilli, turmeric, fenugreek seeds and onion, and cook over medium heat for 5 minutes or until the onion is soft.

Add pumpkin, potato, okra, curry leaves, cinnamon stick and coconut milk. Bring to the boil, reduce heat and simmer, uncovered, for 25–30 minutes or until the vegetables are tender.

REALLY EASY! | 1 HOUR | SERVES 4 | V

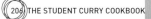

POTATO CURRY

Super-simple and sustaining, this recipe has the added advantage of being inexpensive. Double the quantities for an easy way to feed a crowd.

Boil the potato in water until just tender, then drain

Grind the spring onions, garlic, ginger and chilli to a paste and cook in the ghee for 2 minutes. Add the tomatoes, cinnamon, mustard seeds, garam masala and cardamom and cook for 2–3 minutes, stirring. Add the yoghurt and cook to a thick sauce.

Add the potato and simmer for 4–5 minutes. Stir in the lemon juice if desired. Serve garnished with the reserved spring onion greens.

REALLY EASY!

40 MINUTES

SERVES 4

V

4 large all-purpose potatoes, peeled and cubed

2 spring onions (scallions) (reserve greens for garnish)

2 garlic cloves

1 cm ($^1/_2$ inch) piece ginger

1 green chilli, seeded, chopped

2 tablespoons ghee

2 large tomatoes, chopped

1 small cinnamon stick

$^1/_2$ teaspoon mustard seeds

1 tablespoon garam masala (page 36)

1 cardamom pod, opened

4 tablespoons plain yoghurt or thick (double/heavy) cream

lemon juice, optional

TOOR DAL

500 g (1 lb 2 oz) yellow lentils

5 pieces of kokum, each 5 cm (2 inches) long

2 teaspoons coriander seeds

2 teaspoons cumin seeds

2 tablespoons oil

2 teaspoons black mustard seeds

10 curry leaves

7 whole cloves

10 cm (4 inch) piece cinnamon stick

5 green chillies, finely chopped

Continued →

Kokum is an important ingredient in this dish, with similar souring qualities to tamarind. The sticky, dried purple fruit of the gamboge tree, kokum needs to be soaked briefly before use. It imparts an acidic fruity flavour to a dish. It's available in Indian food shops. There is also a smoked version known as kodampodli.

Soak the lentils in cold water for 2 hours. Rinse the kokum, remove any stones and put in a bowl with cold water for a few minutes to soften. Drain the lentils and place in a heavy-based pan with 1 litre (35 fl oz/4 cups) water and the kokum. Bring slowly to the boil, then simmer for 40 minutes, or until the lentils feel soft when pressed.

Place a small frying pan over low heat and dry-roast the coriander seeds until aromatic. Remove and dry-roast the cumin seeds. Grind the roasted seeds to a fine powder using a spice grinder or mortar and pestle.

Heat the oil in a small pan over low heat. Add the mustard seeds and allow to pop. Add the curry leaves, cloves, cinnamon, chilli, turmeric and the roasted spice mix and cook for 1 minute. Add the tomato and cook for 2–3 minutes, or until the tomato is soft and can be broken up easily. Add the palm sugar, then pour the spicy mixture into the simmering lentils and cook for 10 minutes. Season with salt. Garnish with coriander leaves.

$1/2$ teaspoon ground turmeric

400 g (14 oz) tin chopped tomatoes

20 g ($3/4$ oz) shaved palm sugar (jaggery), or soft brown sugar, or 10 g ($1/4$ oz) molasses

coriander (cilantro) leaves

EASY!

1¼ HOURS + SOAKING TIME

SERVES 8

V

SIDES & SNACKS

Side dishes transform a meal into a feast. Yoghurt-based accompaniments, such as raitas, are traditionally served to counteract the heat or spiciness of curries — yoghurt has a cooling effect. Other side dishes, such as chutneys and pickles, have a very concentrated flavour and only a small amount is needed to enhance the meal. Be selective and choose one side dish or, for a special occasion, make a selection that complement each other.

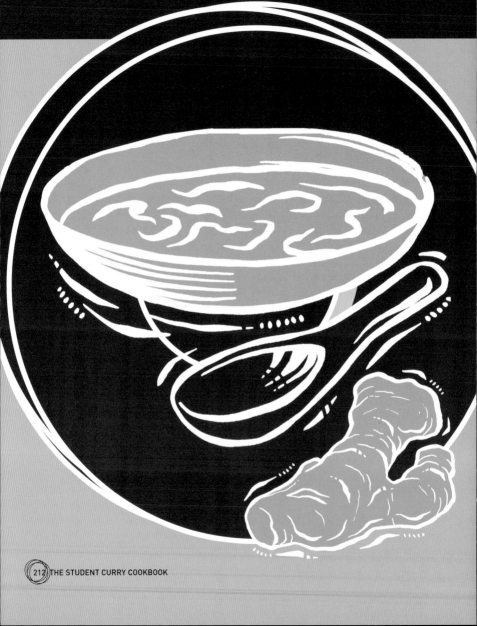

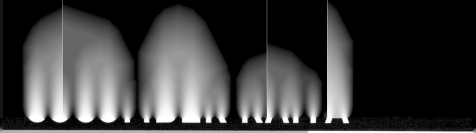

Yoghurt is often a great saviour. It is used in numerous side dishes, specifically to soothe the heat of spicy meals and to refresh the palate. The most famous examples are Indian raitas.

Peel and finely chop the cucumbers and combine with the yoghurt in a small bowl. Set aside.

Fry cumin and mustard seeds in a dry frying pan for 1 minute until fragrant. Add the toasted spices to yoghurt mixture along with the ginger and mix well to combine. Season well with salt and black pepper and garnish with paprika. Serve chilled.

2 Lebanese (short) cucumbers

250 g (9 oz/1 cup) plain yoghurt

1 teaspoon ground cumin

1 teaspoon mustard seeds

$1/2$ teaspoon grated ginger

pinch paprika

REALLY EASY! 10 MINUTES MAKES 2 CUPS √

RAITA

500 g (1 lb 2 oz) telegraph (long) cucumber, grated

1 large, ripe tomato, finely chopped

310 g (11 oz/1¼ cups) plain yoghurt

2 teaspoons oil

1 teaspoon black mustard seeds

1 tablespoon coriander (cilantro) leaves, optional

Freshly made, simple yoghurt preparations known as raitas can include grated vegetables, herbs, spices or coconut — whatever suits the type of curry. Cucumber and tomato are used here.

Put the cucumber and the tomato in a strainer for 20 minutes to drain off any excess liquid. Mix them in a bowl with the yoghurt and then season with salt, to taste.

Heat the oil in a small saucepan over medium heat, add the mustard seeds, then cover and shake the saucepan until the seeds start to pop. Pour seeds and oil over the yoghurt. Serve sprinkled with the coriander leaves.

REALLY EASY! · 15 MINUTES + DRAINING TIME · SERVES 6 · V

CARROT RAITA

Carrots, pistachio nuts and sultanas feature in this recipe. You can vary the taste and texture with other nuts, such as cashews.

Place the chopped pistachio nuts, sultanas and boiling water in a small bowl. Soak for 30 minutes, then drain and pat dry with paper towels.

Place grated carrots, yoghurt, crushed cardamom seeds, ground cumin and chilli powder in another bowl and mix well. Refrigerate for 30 minutes.

Stir the pistachio nut mixture into the yoghurt mixture, keeping a couple of tablespoons aside to garnish. Serve chilled.

35 g (1$\frac{1}{4}$ oz/$\frac{1}{4}$ cup) chopped pistachio nuts

40 g (1$\frac{1}{2}$ oz/$\frac{1}{3}$ cup) sultanas (golden raisins)

4 tablespoons boiling water

2 carrots, grated

185 g (6$\frac{1}{2}$ oz/$\frac{3}{4}$ cup) yoghurt

1 teaspoon crushed cardamom seeds

1 teaspoon ground cumin

$\frac{1}{4}$ teaspoon chilli powder

REALLY EASY!

15 MINUTES + RESTING TIME

SERVES **6**

V

YOGHURT AND MINT RAITA

250 g (9 oz/1 cup) yoghurt

20 g (³/₄ oz/¹/₃ cup) chopped mint

pinch cayenne pepper

In Asian countries, where much of the food is hot and spicy, mint is greatly valued for its cooling properties and sweet, light flavour. This raita has a hint of heat itself, with the inclusion of cayenne.

Combine the yoghurt, mint and cayenne pepper in a small bowl and mix well. Serve chilled.

REALLY EASY!

10 MINUTES

SERVES **6**

V

FRESH MINT RELISH

This relish is simplicity itself. Mint and lemon make a refreshing and lively team and the sugar adds a touch of sweetness to the heat of the chilli.

Finely chop the mint, spring onions and chilli. Mix with the garlic, caster sugar, $1/2$ teaspoon salt and lemon juice. Cover and chill for at least 1 hour.

REALLY EASY!

10 MINUTES + CHILLING TIME

SERVES 6

V

50 g ($1^3/_4$ oz/$2^1/_2$ cups) mint

2 spring onions (scallions)

1 green chilli

1 garlic clove, crushed

1 teaspoon caster (superfine) sugar

2 tablespoons lemon juice

2 tomatoes, diced

3 spring onions (scallions), thinly sliced

2 tablespoons finely chopped coriander (cilantro) leaves

1 green chilli, thinly sliced

1 tablespoon lemon juice

1 teaspoon soft brown sugar

A burst of juicy, ripe tomato on the palate can be just the thing when eating a full-bodied curry. Sweet, cleansing and refreshing, it is a perfect ingredient in a relish.

Combine all the ingredients in a small bowl and season with salt and pepper. Serve chilled.

AUBERGINE PICKLE

The velvety texture of aubergines works well in pickles. This one is characteristically sharp, spicy and robustly flavoured.

Sprinkle the aubergine with salt and leave to stand for 30 minutes.

Meanwhile, place the garlic, ginger, garam masala, turmeric, chilli powder and 1 tablespoon oil in a food processor or blender, and process to a paste.

Rinse the salt off the aubergine and pat dry with paper towels. Heat 4 tablespoons of the oil in a large frying pan, add the aubergine and cook for 5 minutes, or until golden brown. Add the spice paste and cook, stirring, for 2 minutes. Stir in the remaining oil and cook for 10–15 minutes, stirring occasionally. Spoon into clean, warm jars and seal. Store in the refrigerator for up to 5 days.

1 kg (2 lb 4 oz) slender aubergines (eggplants), cut lengthways

6 garlic cloves

1 tablespoon roughly chopped ginger

1 tablespoon garam masala (page 36)

1 teaspoon ground turmeric

1 teaspoon chilli powder

1 tablespoon oil plus 500 ml (17 fl oz/2 cups) oil

REALLY EASY!

35 MINUTES + STANDING TIME

MAKES 2 CUPS

V

LEMON PICKLE

500 g (1 lb 2 oz) thin-skinned lemons

$^1/_2$ teaspoon ground turmeric

$^1/_2$ teaspoon fenugreek seeds

1 teaspoon yellow mustard seeds

$^1/_2$ tablespoon chilli powder

2 tablespoons oil

Pickles are very much a part of an Indian meal. There are many commercially made options available, but a homemade one is far superior.

Wash lemons and place them in a saucepan with 500 ml (17 fl oz/2 cups) water and the turmeric, and bring to the boil, skimming off any impurities. Boil for 8 minutes, remove from the heat and drain well.

Cut each lemon into eight sections and remove the pips. Sprinkle with 2 tablespoons salt and pack into a 500 ml (17 fl oz/2 cup) glass jar which has been sterilized (washed in boiling water and dried in a warm oven). Put the lid on tightly and keep lemons in the jar for 1 week, turning the jar over every day.

Place a small frying pan over low heat and dry-roast fenugreek and mustard seeds until aromatic and starting to pop, shaking the pan occasionally to prevent burning. Grind roasted seeds to a fine powder using a spice grinder or mortar and pestle.

Transfer the lemons to a bowl and mix in ground spices and chilli powder. Clean the jar and sterilize it again. Put the lemons and any juices back into the jar and pour oil over the top. Store in a cool place, or in the fridge after opening.

EASY! · 35 MINUTES + RESTING TIME · MAKES 2 CUPS · V

Wonderfully tangy and aromatic, limes are frequently used in dipping sauces, chutneys and pickles and are often more refreshing than lemon. This dish features lively, sharp flavours.

Cut each limes into 8 thin wedges, sprinkle with salt and set aside.

In a dry frying pan, fry the turmeric, cumin seeds, fennel seeds, fenugreek seeds and mustard seeds for 1–2 minutes. Remove from the heat and grind to a fine powder in a mortar and pestle.

Over a low heat, fry the green chillies, garlic and ginger in 1 tablespoon oil until golden brown. Add the rest of the oil, sugar, lime wedges and spices. Simmer over a low heat for 10 minutes, stirring occasionally. Spoon pickle into warm jars that have been sterilised (washed in boiling water and dried in a warm overn) and seal. Store in the refrigerator.

12 limes

2 teaspoons ground turmeric

2 teaspoons cumin seeds

2 teaspoons fennel seeds

2 teaspoons fenugreek seeds

3 teaspoons brown or yellow mustard seeds

5 green chillies, chopped

4 garlic cloves, sliced

2.5 cm (1 inch) piece ginger, grated

1 tablespoon oil, plus 500 ml (17 fl oz/2 cups) oil

1 tablespoon sugar

REALLY EASY! · 25 MINUTES · MAKES 4–5 CUPS · V

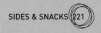

PICKLED GINGER

125 g (4¹/₂ oz) ginger

2 tablespoons sugar

125 ml (4 fl oz/¹/₂ cup) rice vinegar

1 teaspoon grenadine, optional

Ginger is used extensively in Asian cooking. Buy a small amount as and when you need it to ensure freshness. This pickle is sweet, peppery and tangy.

Cut ginger into 2.5 cm (1 inch) pieces. Sprinkle with 2 teaspoons salt, cover and refrigerate for 1 week.

With a very sharp knife, cut into paper-thin slices across the grain. Over low heat dissolve the sugar in the rice vinegar and 2 tablespoons water. Bring to the boil and simmer for 1 minute.

Place the ginger in jars (that have been sterilized (washed in boiling water and dried in a warm oven), cover with the marinade, seal and refrigerate for 1 week before using. The ginger will turn pale pink or it can be coloured using 1 teaspoon grenadine liqueur. Store in the refrigerator for up to 3 months.

REALLY EASY! · 10 MINUTES + CHILLING TIME · SERVES 10 · V

PICKLED VEGETABLES

Pickling began as a way to preserve perishable food for out of season use. The vinegar used in pickling inhibits the growth of bacteria and so preserves the food. These pickles will last for up to 1 month when stored in the refrigerator.

Put the vinegar, sugar and 2 teaspoons of salt into a large non-metallic bowl. Pour over the boiling water, mix well and allow to cool until lukewarm.

Cut the cabbage into 4 cm (1½ inch) strips, then cut the cucumber and carrots into matchsticks. Slice the onion into thick rings.

Add all the vegetables to the warm mixture. Put a flat plate on top of the vegetables. Place a small bowl filled with water on top of plate to weigh it down and submerge vegetables. Leave for 3 days. Place into jars that have been sterilised (washed in boiling water and dried in a warm oven), seal and store in the refrigerator for up to 1 month.

4 tablespoons rice (or clear) vinegar

500ml (17 fl oz/2 cups) boiling water

1 teaspoon sugar

250 g (9 oz) cabbage

1 small Lebanese (short) cucumber

2 carrots

1 white onion

1 tablespoon oil

2 garlic cloves, crushed

1 teaspoon grated ginger

2 cinnamon sticks

4 cloves

1/2 teaspoon chilli powder

1 kg (2 lb 4 oz) fresh or frozen ripe mango flesh, roughly chopped

375 ml (13 fl oz/1 1/2 cups) clear vinegar

220 g (7 3/4 oz/1 cup) sugar

Mangoes are synonymous with summer and their heady fragrance and wonderful flavour are shown to advantage in this chutney. It's not too hot and is very simple to make. Serve with poppadoms.

Heat oil in a heavy-based saucepan over medium heat, add the garlic and ginger and fry for 1 minute. Add the remaining ingredients and bring to the boil.

Reduce the heat to low and cook for 1 hour, or until the mango is thick and pulpy, like jam. It should fall in sheets off the spoon when ready. Add salt, to taste, and more chilli, if you want more heat. Remove the whole spices.

Pour chutney into hot sterilized jars (wash the jars in boiling water and dry them thoroughly in a warm oven). Seal the jars and allow to cool completely. Store in a cool place, or in the fridge after opening.

EASY!   1 1/4 HOURS   MAKES 2 CUPS   V

MINT AND CORIANDER CHUTNEY

This aromatic mint and coriander chutney is perfect for serving with samosas or singharas. That said, it can be served with just about any Indian meal. Yoghurt adds a creamy texture.

Wash the mint and the coriander leaves. Discard any tough stems but keep all of the young soft ones for flavour.

Blend all ingredients and $^{1}/_{2}$ teaspoon of salt together in a blender or food processor, or chop everything finely and pound it together in a mortar and pestle.

Taste the chutney and add more salt, if necessary. If you prefer a creamier, milder chutney, stir in more yoghurt.

30 g (1 oz/1$^{1}/_{2}$ cups) mint leaves

30 g (1 oz/1 cup) coriander (cilantro) leaves

1 green chilli

1 tablespoon tamarind paste

1$^{1}/_{2}$ teaspoons sugar

3 tablespoons plain yoghurt, optional

REALLY EASY! · **15** MINUTES · SERVES **4** · V

FRESH COCONUT CHUTNEY

1 teaspoon chana dal

1 teaspoon urad dal

$^1/_2$ fresh coconut, grated

2 green chillies, seeded, finely chopped

1 tablespoon oil

1 teaspoon black mustard seeds

5 curry leaves

1 teaspoon tamarind paste

In India, chutney made with fresh coconut is served with idlis and dosas for breakfast, or as a snack. The curry leaves and tamarind give a distinctive Indian flavour.

Soak the dals in cold water for 2 hours. Drain well.

Put the grated coconut, chillies and $^1/_2$ teaspoon salt in a food processor and blend to a fine paste. Alternatively, finely chop everything together with a knife or pound with a mortar and pestle.

Heat the oil in a small saucepan and add the mustard seeds and dals, then cover and shake the saucepan until they start to pop. Add the curry leaves and fry for 1 minute, or until the dal browns. Add these ingredients to the coconut with the tamarind; mix well.

REALLY EASY!

10 MINUTES + SOAKING TIME

SERVES 4

V

PINEAPPLE CHUTNEY

This quick and simple fresh pineapple chutney can be enjoyed as part of any main meal including meat and poultry or fish and seafood dishes. The acidity of the pineapple will cut through any rich dishes and make a refreshing contrast.

Peel the pineapple by cutting down the outside in strips. Remove any remaining eyes, then slice the pineapple lengthways and remove the tough central core.

Rub the pineapple with 1 teaspoon salt and allow it to rest for a few minutes in a colander to draw out some of the juices. Rinse, then chop into small chunks and drain well on paper towels.

Mix all ingredients together in a bowl, adding enough sugar, lime juice, pepper and salt to achieve a balanced flavour. Chill and serve.

Note: To make 2 tablespoons of ginger juice, take a 5 cm (2 inch) piece of ginger and pound it in a mortar and pestle or grate with a fine grater into a bowl. Put the ginger into a piece of muslin (cheesecloth), twist it up tightly and squeeze out all the juice.

2 small or 1 large pineapple(s), slightly green

1 red onion, thinly sliced into half rings

4 red chillies, seeded, finely chopped

4 garlic cloves, finely chopped

2 teaspoons ginger juice (see Note)

3 tablespoons icing (confectioners') sugar, or to taste

6 tablespoons lime juice, or to taste

SWEET TOMATO CHUTNEY

8 garlic cloves, roughly chopped

5 cm (2 inch) piece of ginger, roughly chopped

800 g (1 lb 12 oz) peeled fresh tomatoes

310 ml (10¾ fl oz/ 1¼ cups) clear vinegar

350 g (12 oz) palm sugar (jaggery), or soft brown sugar

2 tablespoons sultanas (golden raisins)

2 teaspoons salt

¾ teaspoon cayenne pepper

chilli powder, (optional)

This is an easy store-cupboard chutney. It is an especially handy recipe if you have an abundance of very ripe tomatoes. If you can't find clear vinegar at Indian food shops or supermarkets, you can use white vinegar instead.

Combine the garlic, ginger and half the tomatoes in a blender or food processor and blend until smooth. If you don't have a blender, crush the garlic, grate the ginger and push the tomatoes through a sieve before mixing them together.

Put remaining tomatoes, vinegar, sugar, sultanas and 2 teaspons salt in a heavy-based saucepan. Bring to the boil and add garlic and ginger mixture. Reduce heat and simmer gently for 1½–1¾ hours, stirring occasionally, until mixture is thick enough to fall off a spoon in sheets. Make sure the mixture doesn't catch on the bottom of the saucepan.

Add the cayenne pepper. For a hotter chutney, add a little chilli powder. Allow to cool, then pour into sterilized jars (wash two 250 ml (9 fl oz/1 cup) jars in boiling water and dry them in a warm oven). Store in the fridge after opening.

EASY! · 2¼ HOURS · MAKES 2 CUPS · V

CARROT SALAD

Carrot salads are popular throughout India. In this one, the spices are heated in the oil in order for their flavour to permeate the dressing. The salad gets more flavoursome if it is allowed to stand for at least half an hour before serving.

Heat the oil in a small saucepan over medium heat, add the mustard and cumin seeds, then cover and shake the saucepan until the seeds start to pop.

Add the turmeric, $1/4$ teaspoon salt and sugar to the saucepan, then remove the saucepan from the heat and allow the spices to cool for 5 minutes. Mix in the lemon juice, then toss the carrots through. Cover and leave for 30 minutes.

1 tablespoon oil

$1/4$ teaspoon black mustard seeds

$1/4$ teaspoon cumin seeds

pinch ground turmeric

$1^1/2$ tablespoons lemon juice

500 g (1 lb 2 oz) carrots, finely grated

REALLY EASY!

15 MINUTES + RESTING TIME

SERVES **4**

V

POTATO MASALA

2 tablespoons oil

1 teaspoon black mustard seeds

10 curry leaves

1/4 teaspoon ground turmeric

1 cm (1/2 inch) piece ginger, grated

2 green chillies, finely chopped

2 onions, chopped

500 g (1 lb 2 oz) waxy potatoes, cut into 2.5 cm (1 inch) cubes

1 tablespoon tamarind paste

This filling is traditionally rolled in dosas (a type of crisp pancake) to make masala dosa, which is served for breakfast or as a snack in Southern India. It also makes an excellent spicy side dish.

Heat the oil in a heavy-based frying pan, add the mustard seeds, cover and when they pop add the curry leaves, turmeric, ginger, chillies and onions and cook, uncovered, until the onions are soft.

Add the potato cubes and 250 ml (9 fl oz/1 cup) water to the pan, bring to a boil, cover and cook until the potatoes are tender and almost breaking up. If there is any liquid left in the pan, simmer, uncovered, until it evaporates. If the potatoes aren't cooked and there is no liquid left, add a little more and continue to cook. Add tamarind and season with salt to taste.

REALLY EASY! 30 MINUTES SERVES 4 V

This is a refreshing side dish, traditionally used as an accompaniment to biryani, but it is versatile and can be served with most dishes. Yoghurt and buttermilk have a cooling effect when churri is eaten with hot or spicy dishes.

Place a small frying pan over low heat and dry-roast the cumin seeds until aromatic. Grind the seeds to a fine powder in a spice grinder or pestle and mortar.

Chop the mint, coriander, ginger and chillies to a fine paste in a blender, or chop together finely with a knife. Add the yoghurt and buttermilk and a pinch of salt to the mixture and blend until all the ingredients are well mixed. Check the seasoning, adjust if necessary, then mix in the sliced onion and the ground cumin, reserving a little cumin to sprinkle on top.

Note: If you can't find buttermilk, mix 310 ml (10³/₄ fl oz/1¹/₄ cups) milk with 1¹/₄ tablespoons lemon juice and let rest for a few minutes before using.

1 teaspoon cumin seeds

10 g (¹/₄ oz/¹/₂ cup) mint, roughly chopped

15 g (¹/₂ oz/¹/₂ cup) coriander (cilantro) leaves, roughly chopped

2.5 cm (1 inch) piece ginger, roughly chopped

2 green chillies, roughly chopped

310 g (11 oz/1¹/₄ cups) plain yoghurt

310 ml (10³/₄ fl oz/ 1¹/₄ cups) buttermilk (see Note)

1 onion, thinly sliced

DHAL

200 g (7 oz) red lentils

4 cm (1 1/2 inch) piece fresh
ginger, cut into 3 slices

1/2 teaspoon ground
turmeric

3 tablespoons ghee or oil

2 garlic cloves, crushed

1 onion, finely chopped

pinch of asafoetida,
optional

1 teaspoon cumin seeds

1 teaspoon ground
coriander

1/4 teaspoon chilli powder

In India, dhal refers to both the dried pulse and
the finished dish. In this recipe, lentils are used,
but chickpeas and other peas are also popular.
To bolster the simple flavour of the lentils, spices
such as cumin and asafoetida are fried in ghee,
releasing their earthy aromas.

Place lentils and 1 litre (35 fl oz/4 cups) water in a
medium saucepan, and bring to the boil. Turn the
heat to low, add ginger and turmeric, and simmer,
covered, for 1 hour or until lentils are tender. Stir
every 5 minutes during the last 30 minutes to stop
the lentils sticking to the pan. Remove the ginger
and stir in 1/2 teaspoon salt.

Heat the ghee in a frying pan; add the garlic and
onion, and cook over medium heat for 3 minutes
or until the onion is golden. Add the asafoetida, if
using, cumin seeds, coriander and chilli powder,
and cook for 2 minutes.

Add the onion mixture to the lentils and stir gently
to combine.

REALLY EASY! · 1 1/4 HOURS · SERVES 4-6 · V

AUBERGINE SAMBAL

Aubergine is also known by its Indian name, brinjal. For this recipe, it is preferable to use the long, thin, Asian aubergine. Use the sambal as an accompaniment or eat it as a dip with pieces of Indian bread.

Preheat the oven to 200°C (400°F/Gas 6). Slice each aubergine in half and brush the cut halves with the oil and the ground turmeric. Place aubergines in a roasting tin and roast for 30 minutes, or until they are browned all over and very soft.

Scoop the aubergine pulp into a bowl. Mash pulp with the lime juice, chillies and onion, reserving some chilli and onion for garnish. Season with salt to taste, then fold in the yoghurt. Garnish with coriander leaves and remaining onion and chilli.

2 aubergines (eggplants)

2 teaspoons oil

1/2 teaspoon ground turmeric

3 tablespoons lime juice

2 red chillies, seeded, finely diced

1 small red onion, finely diced

4 tablespoons plain yoghurt

1 tablespoon chopped coriander (cilantro) leaves

REALLY EASY! 45 MINUTES SERVES 4 V

CURRY PUFFS WITH YOGHURT AND MINT

2 tablespoons oil

1 tablespoon curry powder

250 g (9 oz) minced (ground) pork

165 g (5¾ oz/1 cup) finely chopped potato

155 g (5½ oz/1 cup) finely chopped jap pumpkin (kent squash)

155 g (5½ oz/1 cup) finely chopped carrot

2 tablespoons chopped spring onions (scallions)

1 large brown onion, chopped

4 sheets frozen puff pastry

YOGHURT AND MINT SAUCE

375 g (13 oz/1½ cups) plain yoghurt

3 tablespoons chopped mint

2 garlic cloves, crushed

Curry puffs originated in Malaysia, and are common throughout Asia. The yoghurt and mint sauce is a fresh and tasty accompaniment.

Preheat the oven to 220°C (425°F/Gas 7). Brush two oven trays with melted butter or oil. Heat the oil in a frying pan and cook the curry powder, stirring, for 1 minute. Add the pork and cook over high heat for 5 minutes, until browned. Break up any lumps with a fork as it cooks.

Add the vegetables; cook, stirring, for 2 minutes. Add 125 ml (4 fl oz/½ cup) water, reduce the heat to medium, and cook, covered, until the vegetables are tender. Remove the lid and cook until any liquid has evaporated. Season well and set aside to cool.

Cut 4 triangles out of each pastry sheet. Divide the mixture between triangles. Fold over and press the edges together, pinching in a fluted pattern to seal. Place the puffs onto trays and bake for 20 minutes, until puffed and golden brown.

Make yoghurt and mint sauce by whisking all the ingredients in a bowl. Season with salt and freshly ground black pepper.

EASY! 1½ HOURS MAKES 16

VEGETABLE BHAJI

These deep-fried vegetables make an excellent snack or starter. In India, street vendors at their stalls line the busy streets, selling an astonishing variety of such items to passersby. The busier the stall, the tastier the snack.

Cut the vegetables into thin sticks. Combine the besan flour, chilli powder, turmeric, asafoetida and a pinch of salt. Add enough water to make a thick batter that will hold the vegetables together. Mix the vegetables and curry leaves into the batter.

Fill a karhai or heavy-based saucepan one-third full with oil and heat to 180°C (350°F) (a cube of bread will brown in 15 seconds). Lift clumps of vegetables out of the batter and lower carefully into the oil. Fry until golden all over and cooked through, then drain on paper towels. Sprinkle with salt and serve hot with chutney or raita.

100 g (3 1/2 oz) carrots

100 g (3 1/2 oz) snow peas (mangetout)

50 g (1 3/4 oz) thin aubergines (eggplants)

220 g (7 3/4 oz/2 cups) besan (chickpea flour)

1 teaspoon chilli powder

1 teaspoon ground turmeric

1/4 teaspoon asafoetida

6 curry leaves

oil, for deep-frying

EASY! | **30** MINUTES | MAKES **20** | V

10 small green bananas

oil, for deep-frying

ground turmeric, optional

These chips, along with roasted fried peanuts, are sold by Indian vendors who stroll the streets with large baskets balanced on their heads.

Oil your hands before you start, or wear disposable gloves, as a thick, sticky sap will be given off by the unripe bananas. Using a knife or mandolin, cut bananas into 5 mm ($^1/_4$ inch) thick slices, oiling the blade if it gets sticky.

Fill a karhai or heavy-based saucepan one-third full with oil and heat to 180°C (350°F) (a cube of bread will brown in 15 seconds). Put sliced bananas directly into the hot oil in batches and stir while the chips cook. After 1 or 2 minutes, put in 1 teaspoon of salt (the oil will not splutter). You will need to do this for the first batch, then for every second batch.

Remove banana chips when golden brown, drain on paper towels and toss in ground turmeric.

Store the banana chips in an airtight container when completely cold. If the chips are not cooled completely, they will go soggy. They will keep for 2 weeks but may need refreshing after 10 days. Do this by heating them in a hot oven, or under a grill (broiler), until crisp.

EASY! · 15 MINUTES · SERVES 8 · V

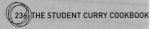

ALOO KI TIKKI

These potato patties are sold at street food stalls in Northern India. There are many variations and they are served with different chutneys such as mint and coriander or tamarind. They can be eaten as a starter or a snack.

Cook the potatoes in boiling water for 15 minutes, or until tender enough to mash. Drain well until they are dry but still hot. Cook the peas in boiling water for 4 minutes, or until tender, then drain.

Mash the potato in a large bowl and add the peas. Put 1 tablespoon of the oil in a small saucepan and fry the chilli, onion, ginger and spices for 1 minute, or until aromatic. Add them to the potato with the besan flour and mix. Mix in lemon juice and some salt. Divide the potato into portions the size of golf balls and shape into patties.

Heat remaining oil in a heavy-based frying pan (non-stick if you have one) and add potato patties in batches. Fry them on each side until crisp and golden brown. Serve hot or cold in small dishes.

500 g (1 lb 2 oz) potatoes, cut into pieces

155 g (5^1/$_2$ oz/1 cup) fresh or frozen peas

4 tablespoons oil

2 green chillies, finely chopped

^{1}/$_2$ red onion, finely chopped

2 cm (^{3}/$_4$ inch) piece ginger, grated

1 teaspoon ground turmeric

1 teaspoon ground cumin

1 teaspoon ground coriander

^{1}/$_2$ teaspoon garam masala (page 36)

2 tablespoons besan (chickpea flour)

1 tablespoon lemon juice

EASY! **45** MINUTES · MAKES **24** · V

90 g (3¹/₄ oz/¹/₂ cup) rice flour

4 tablespoons cashew nuts

75 g (2¹/₂ oz/²/₃ cup) besan (chickpea flour)

pinch bicarbonate of soda

10 curry leaves, chopped

4 green chillies, seeded, finely chopped

2 cm (³/₄ inch) piece ginger, finely chopped

1 red onion, finely chopped

1 tablespoon ghee

oil, for deep-frying

These are deep-fried nibbles enjoyed as tea-time snacks. They are known by different names in different areas and have regional idiosyncrasies, including their shape and the types of flour and flavourings used in the batter.

Place a small frying pan over low heat and dry-roast the rice flour until it turns light brown. Dry-roast the cashew nuts in the same pan until they brown, then finely chop them. Mix the rice flour with the besan flour, then add the bicarbonate of soda and a pinch of salt. Add the cashew nuts, curry leaves, green chilli, ginger, onion and ghee. Mix together well, adding a few drops of water, if necessary, to make a stiff dough. Form dough into 20 small balls.

Fill a karhai or heavy-based saucepan one-third full with ghee or oil and heat to 180°C (350°F) (a cube of bread will brown in 15 seconds). Fry five or six balls at a time until golden brown, then drain each batch on paper towels.

EASY! 25 MINUTES MAKES 20 V

NIMKI

These are small, deep-fried pieces of dough served as a snack. The nigella give these tidbits a pungent, distinctive taste and aroma. In India, they are sold at sweet shops where they also sell nuts and other savouries. Serve with mint and coriander chutney.

Sift the maida and 1 teaspoon salt into a bowl and add the nigella seeds. Rub in the ghee until the mixture resembles breadcrumbs. Add about 125 ml (4 fl oz/^{1}/$_2$ cup) water, a little at a time, to make a pliable dough. Turn the dough out onto a floured surface and knead for 5 minutes, or until smooth, then cover and rest it for 10 minutes. Don't refrigerate the dough or the ghee will harden.

Divide dough into two portions and roll out each portion until about 3 mm (^{1}/$_8$ inch) thick. Cut them into 1 cm (^{1}/$_2$ inch) wide strips, then into diamonds about 3 cm (1^1/$_4$ inch) long, by making diagonal cuts along the strips. Prick the diamonds with a fork.

Fill a karhai or heavy-based saucepan one-third full with oil and heat to about 170°C/325°F (a cube of bread will brown in 20 seconds). Fry the nimki in batches until light golden and crisp and then drain on paper towels.

250 g (9 oz/2 cups) maida or plain (all-purpose) flour

1 teaspoon nigella seeds

1 tablespoon ghee

oil, for deep-frying

EASY! · 30 MINUTES + RESTING TIME · MAKES 60 · V

CHUCUMBER

1 red onion, finely chopped

2 small cucumbers, about 200 g (7 oz), finely chopped

about 100 g (3$^{1}/_{2}$ oz) ripe tomatoes, finely chopped

3 tablespoons finely chopped coriander (cilantro)

1 red chilli, finely chopped

1 green chilli, finely chopped

1$^{1}/_{2}$ tablespoons lemon juice

1 teaspoon oil

125 g (4$^{1}/_{2}$ oz/$^{3}/_{4}$ cup) peanuts, roughly chopped

1$^{1}/_{2}$ teaspoons chaat masala (page 35)

This is a healthy North Indian snack, often served as a starter in restaurants, or with drinks. Many of the ingredients can be increased or decreased according to personal taste. The combination of cucumber and fresh coriander makes this a very refreshing snack.

Stir the onion, cucumber, tomato, coriander, chillies and lemon juice together in a bowl.

Heat the oil in a heavy-based frying pan over high heat, add the peanuts and 1 teaspoon salt and fry for 1 minute. Sprinkle with $^{1}/_{2}$ teaspoon ground black pepper and the chaat masala and then stir fry for 2 minutes. Remove from the heat and add to the onion mixture. Season with more salt, to taste, before serving The seasoning is added at the end to prevent the ingredients releasing too much juice before serving.

Serve chucumber in small bowls. It can be eaten with a spoon or alternatively scooped up in pieces of roti or poppadoms.

EASY! 20 MINUTES SERVES 4 V

VEGETABLE PAKORAS

These are ideal as a starter, or can be served as a main course with a curry or fresh tomato sauce, spiked with chilli.

Boil the potato until just tender, and then peel and chop finely.

Chop cauliflower, capsicum and onion finely. Shred the cabbage or spinach.

Make a creamy batter of the remaining ingredients with cold water. Add vegetables and mix in evenly.

Heat oil. Drop tablespoonful of the mixture into the oil, about eight at a time, to fry until golden brown. Remove to a rack covered with paper towels.

Serve hot with the sweet mango chutney and tamarind sauce.

Note: Shallow-fry the mixture as larger patties.

1 large potato

1 small cauliflower

1 small red capsicum (pepper)

1 onion

2 cabbage or 5 spinach leaves

100 g (3^1/$_2$ oz/^{1}/$_2$ cup) corn kernels, parboiled

2 teaspoons garam masala (page 36)

2 teaspoons ground coriander

165 g (5^3/$_4$ oz/1^1/$_2$ cups) besan (chickpea flour)

3 tablespoons flour

1 teaspoon bicarbonate of soda

1 teaspoon chilli powder

1 tablespoon lemon juice

oil, for deep-frying

BREADS

Breads are a great accompaniment to many curries. The breads in this book are all Indian in origin so would go better with Indian-style curries but there is no need to limit yourself. Use breads to scoop up the curry — you'll find this easier with more 'dry' curries.

yoghurt

NAAN

This is perhaps the most famous leavened bread from north India. Traditionally, it is cooked on the tray of a tandoor (clay) oven. It is not easy to create the intense heat in a domestic oven, so the texture will be slightly different but the taste still delicious.

Preheat oven to 200°C (400°F/Gas 6). Grease two baking trays 28 x 32 cm (11¼ x 12¾ inch) lightly. Sift together flour, baking powder, bicarbonate of soda and 1 teaspoon salt. Mix in the beaten egg, melted ghee or butter, yoghurt and gradually add enough of the milk to form a soft. Cover with a damp cloth and leave in a warm place for 2 hours.

Knead dough for 2–3 minutes, or until smooth, on a well-floured surface. Divide into 8 even portions and roll each one into an oval 15 cm (6 inches) long. Brush with water and place, wet side down, on the prepared baking trays. Brush with melted ghee or butter and then bake for 8–10 minutes, or until golden brown.

500 g (1 lb 2 oz/4 cups) plain (all-purpose) flour

1 teaspoon baking powder

½ teaspoon bicarbonate of soda (baking soda)

1 egg, beaten

1 tablespoon ghee or butter

125 g (4½ oz/½ cup) plain yoghurt

about 250 ml (9 fl oz/ 1 cup) milk

EASY! · 35 MINUTES + RESTING TIME · MAKES 8 · V

CHAPATI

280 g (10 oz/2¼ cups)
chapati flour

Chapatis are the most basic form of unleavened bread. They should be cooked on a high heat to prevent them becoming tough. You can use equal amounts of wholemeal (whole wheat) flour and maida flour if you can't buy chapati flour.

Put the flour in a large bowl with a pinch of salt. Slowly add 250 ml (9 fl oz/1 cup) water, or enough to form a firm dough. Put on a lightly floured surface and knead until smooth. Cover with plastic wrap and leave for 50 minutes.

Divide into 14 portions and roll into 14 cm (5½ inch) circles. Heat a frying pan over medium heat and brush with melted ghee or oil. Cook chapatis one at a time, flattening the surface, for 2–3 minutes on each side, or until they are golden brown and bubbles start appearing.

EASY! · 30 MINUTES + RESTING TIME · MAKES 14 · V

PARATHAS

This fried, unleavened bread is often eaten on special occasions. It's best cooked on a tava or iron griddle. You can use equal amounts of wholemeal (whole wheat) and maida flours if you can't buy chapati flour.

280 g (10 oz/2¼ cups) chapati flour

40 g (1½ oz) ghee

melted ghee or oil

Place the flour and a pinch of salt in a large bowl. Rub in the ghee with your fingertips until fine and crumbly. Make a well in the centre and gradually add 185 ml (6 fl oz/¾ cup) cold water to form a firm dough. Turn onto a well-floured surface and knead until smooth. Cover with plastic wrap and set aside for 40 minutes.

Divide into 10 portions. Roll each portion on a floured surface to a 13 cm (5 inch) circle. Brush lightly with melted ghee or oil. Cut through each round to the centre and roll tightly to form a cone shape, then press down on the pointed top. Re-roll into a 13 cm (5 inch) circle again.

Cook one at a time in hot oil or ghee in a frying pan until puffed and lightly browned on both sides. Drain on paper towels.

REALLY EASY! · 35 MINUTES + RESTING TIME · MAKES 10 · V

STUFFED PARATHAS

400 g (14 oz/4 cups) chapati flour)

4 tablespoons oil or ghee

250 g (9 oz) potatoes, unpeeled

1/4 teaspoon mustard seeds

1/2 onion, finely chopped

pinch ground turmeric

pinch asafoetida

ghee or oil, for shallow-frying

extra ghee or oil, for brushing on the dough

Stuffed parathas are very much a festive food. After stuffing them, roll them out carefully so the filling doesn't ooze out. If you can't get hold of chapati flour, you can use equal amounts of wholemeal (whole-wheat) and maida flours.

Sift the flour and 1 teaspoon salt into a bowl and make a well in the centre. Add 2 tablespoons of the oil or ghee and about 310 ml (10³/4 fl oz/1¹/4 cups) tepid water and mix to a soft, pliable dough. Turn out onto a floured surface, knead for 5 minutes, then place in an oiled bowl. Cover and allow to rest for 30 minutes.

Simmer potatoes for 15–20 minutes or until cooked. Cool slightly, then peel and mash. Heat remaining oil or ghee in a saucepan over medium heat, add the mustard seeds, cover and shake the saucepan until seeds start to pop. Add onion and fry 1 minute. Stir in the turmeric and asafoetida. Mix in potatoes and cook for 1–2 minutes over low heat, or until mixture leaves the side of the saucepan. Season with salt to taste, and allow to cool.

Divide the dough into 14 portions and roll each into a 15 cm (6 inch) circle. Spread 1 teaspoon of the potato filling evenly over one half of each circle of dough and fold into a semicircle. Rub oil on half the surface area, then fold over into quarters. Roll out until doubled in size. Cover the parathas with a cloth, then cook them one at a time.

Heat a tava, griddle or a heavy-bottomed frying pan over medium heat. Oil the surface of the tava or griddle. Remove the excess flour on each paratha prior to cooking by holding it in the palms of your hands and gently slapping it from one hand to the other. If you leave the flour on it may burn.

Cook each paratha for 2–3 minutes, then turn over and cook for 1 minute, or until the surface has brown flecks. Cooking should be quick to ensure the parathas remain soft. Cover the cooked parathas with a cloth. Parathas must be served warm. They can be reheated in a microwave, or wrapped in aluminium foil and heated in a conventional oven at 180°C (350°F/Gas 4) for 10 minutes.

EASY! | 1 HOUR + RESTING TIME | MAKES 14 | V

DOSAS

110 g (3³/₄ oz/¹/₂ cup)
urad dal

1 teaspoon salt

260 g (9¹/₄ oz/1³/₄ cups)
rice flour

oil, or ghee for cooking

Large, spongy, rice pancakes with a crisp surface. dosas are eaten with sambhar, a spicy vegetable dish, for breakfast. For the best result, rice flour that is specially made for making dosas should be used as it is ground to the right consistency.

Put the dal in a bowl and cover with water. Soak for at least 4 hours or overnight.

Drain, then grind the dal with the salt and a little water in a food processor, blender or mortar and pestle to form a fine paste. Mix the paste with the rice flour, add 1 litre (35 fl oz/4 cups) water and mix well. Cover with a cloth and leave in a warm place for 8 hours, or until the batter ferments and bubbles. The batter will double in volume.

Heat a tava or a non-stick frying pan over medium heat and leave to heat up. Don't overheat it—the heat should always be medium. Lightly brush the surface of the tava or frying pan with oil. Stir the batter and pour a ladleful into the middle of the griddle and quickly spread it out with the back of the ladle or a flexible-bladed knife, to form a thin pancake. Don't worry if the dosa is not perfect— they are very hard to get exactly right. Drizzle a little oil or ghee around the edge to help it crisp up. Cook until small holes appear on the surface and the edges start to curl. Turn over with a spatula and cook other side. (The first dosa is often a disaster but it will season the pan for the following ones.)

Repeat with the remaining mixture, oiling the pan between each dosa. Roll the dosas into big tubes and keep warm. Dosas are often filled with potato masala filling (page 230) and served with chutneys, or with curries.

EASY! · 30 MINUTES + RESTING TIME · MAKES 20 · V

375 g (13 oz/2½ cups) wholemeal (whole-wheat) flour

1 tablespoon ghee or oil

ghee or oil, for deep-frying

pinch salt

Puris are simple to make even for a large group of people. The dough should be prepared ahead of time and allowed to rest. The oil should be hot so the puris puff up well, but not so hot that you burn the outside and undercook the inside.

Sift together the flour and a pinch of salt. Using your fingertips, rub in 1 tablespoon ghee or oil. Gradually add 250 ml (9 fl oz/1 cup) water to form a firm dough. Knead on a lightly floured surface until smooth. Cover with plastic wrap and set aside for 50 minutes.

Divide into 18 portions and roll each into a 14 cm (5½ inch) circle. Heat 3 cm (1¼ inch) oil in a deep frying pan until moderately hot; fry one at a time, spooning oil over until they puff up and swell. Cook on each side until golden brown. Drain on paper towels. Serve immediately.

EASY! · 30 MINUTES + RESTING TIME · MAKES 18 · V

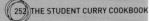

ROTI

Sift flour into a large bowl with 1 teaspoon salt. Rub in ghee or oil with your fingertips. Add the egg and 250 ml (9 fl oz/1 cup) warm water, and mix together with a flat-bladed knife to form a moist dough.

Turn out on to a well-floured surface and knead for 10 minutes, or until you have a soft dough. Sprinkle with more flour as necessary. Form dough into a ball and brush with oil. Place in a bowl, cover and rest for 2 hours.

Working on a lightly-floured bench top, divide the dough into 12 pieces and roll into even-sized balls. Take one ball and with a little oil on your fingertips, hold it in the air and work around the edge pulling out dough until a 2 mm x 15 cm ($\frac{1}{16}$ x 6 inch) round is formed. Lay on a lightly-floured surface and cover with plastic wrap to prevent it drying out. Repeat process with the remaining balls.

Heat a large frying pan over high heat and brush it with ghee or oil. Carefully place one roti in frying pan, brush with some extra beaten egg and cook for 1 minute, or until underside is golden. Slide onto a plate and brush pan with more ghee or oil. Cook other side of roti for 50–60 seconds, or until golden. Remove from pan and cover to keep warm.

375 g (13 oz/3 cups) roti or plain (all-purpose) flour

2 tablespoons softened ghee or oil

1 egg, lightly beaten

REALLY EASY! · 45 MINUTES + RESTING TIME · MAKES 12 · V

GLOSSARY

asafoetida This yellowish powder or lump of resin is made from the dried latex of a type of fennel. Asafoetida has an extremely pungent smell. It is used to make pulses and legumes more digestible. Asafoetida is always fried to calm its aroma.

aubergine (eggplant) There are lots of varieties of aubergine used in Asian cuisine and, unlike in the West, bitterness is a prized quality. Common aubergines include the Thai, long and pea varieties. Cut aubergines using a stainless steel knife and store in salted water to prevent from turning black.

bamboo shoots The young, pale shoots of certain types of bamboo, which have a mellow flavour. Fresh ones require some time-consuming preparation before use, but it's easier to use the tinned ones as they are.

besan (chickpea flour) Also known as gram flour, this is a yellow flour made from ground Bengal gram or chickpeas. It has a nutty flavour and is used as a thickener in curries, as well as in batters, dumplings, sweets and breads.

cardamom Dry green pods full of sticky, tiny brown or black seeds which have a sweet flavour and pungent aroma. If you need ground cardamom, open the pods and grind the seeds.

Ready-ground cardamom quickly loses flavour. Use pods whole or crushed.

cayenne pepper A very hot red chilli powder that is made from sun-dried red chillies.

chapati flour Sometimes called atta, this is made from finely ground whole durum wheat. Some have a proportion of white flour added. This is much finer and softer than wholemeal (wholewheat) flour so if you can't find it, use half wholemeal and half maida or plain (all-purpose) flour.

chaat masala Seasoning used for various snacks known as chaat. The spice blend uses a variety of flavourings including asafoetida, amchoor, black salt, cumin, cayenne, ajowan and pepper.

chickpeas Chickpeas can be white or black. The white chickpeas are actually a tan colour and the black ones are dark brown. Usually sold whole, but also sold split, dried chickpeas need to be soaked for 8 hours in cold water before use. They will double in size. Tinned ones can be used but need to be added at the end of the cooking time as they are already very soft.

chillies Recipes generally give a colour (red or green), rather than a variety.

The small bird's eye chillies are usually the hottest.

chillies, dried Dried whole chillies of various shapes, sizes and heat levels. Sometimes soaked to soften them. Remove the seeds if they are very hot.

chilli flakes Dried, coarsely ground chillies with the chilli seeds included; usually hot.

chilli powder A wide variety of chillies are dried and crushed to make chilli powders. Some, such as Kashmiri chilli powder and paprika, are used for colour, whereas others like cayenne are used for heat. Don't use chilli powder indiscriminately. The amount used can be varied, to taste, so start with a small amount and determine how hot it is.

cloves the dried, unopened flower buds of the clove tree. They are brown and nail-shaped and have a pungent flavour, so use in moderation. Use whole or ground.

coconut The fruit of a coconut palm. The inner nut is encased in a husk which has to be removed. The hard shell can then be drained of juice and cracked open to extract white meat. Coconut meat is jellyish in younger nuts and harder in older ones. Dried coconut meat is known as copra.

coconut cream made by soaking fresh, grated coconut in boiling water and squeezing out a thick, sweet coconut-flavoured liquid. Available tinned.

coconut milk A thinner version of coconut cream, made as above but with more water or from a second pressing. Available tinned.

coriander (cilantro) Fresh coriander leaves are used in recipes and as a garnish. Buy healthy bunches of green leaves and avoid any that are yellowing.

coriander seeds The round seeds of the coriander plant. The seeds have a spicy aroma and are common in spice mixes such as garam masala. To intensify the flavour, dry-roast the seeds until aromatic, before crushing them. Best freshly ground for each dish. Available whole or ground.

cumin seeds The green or ochre, elongated ridged seeds of a plant of the parsley family. It has a peppery, slightly bitter flavour and is aromatic. To intensify flavour, dry-roast seeds before crushing them. Best freshly ground for each dish.

curry leaves Smallish green aromatic leaves of a tree native to India and Sri Lanka. These give a distinctive flavour and are usually fried and added to the dish or used as a garnish at the end.

dal (dhal) is used to describe not only an ingredient but a dish made from it. In India, dal relates to any type of dried split pea, bean or lentil. A dal dish can be a thin soup or more like a stew. All dal should be rinsed before use.

dried shrimp These are tiny, orange, saltwater shrimps that have been dried in the sun. They come in different sizes and really small ones have their heads and shells still attached. Dried shrimp need to be soaked in water or rice wine to soften them before use. Use as a seasoning, not as a main ingredient.

fennel seeds The dried seeds of a Mediterranean plant, which are oval, greenish yellow, with ridges running along them, and look like large cumin. Used as an aromatic and a digestive. To intensify flavour, dry-roast seeds before crushing them. Available whole or ground. Best freshly ground.

fenugreek leaves The leaves of young fenugreek plants, used as a vegetable and treated much like English spinach, which can be used as a substitute. They have a mildly bitter flavour. Strip the leaves off the stalks before using. Available fresh or dried.

fenugreek seeds Not a true seed, but a dried legume. Ochre in colour and almost square, with a groove down one side, fenugreek has a curry aroma (it is a major ingredient in commercial curry powders) and is best dry-roasted for a few seconds before use. Don't brown them too much or they will be bitter.

fish sauce Made from salted anchovy-like fish that are left to break down naturally in the heat, fish sauce is literally the liquid that is drained off. It varies in quality.

galangal A rhizome, similar to ginger, used extensively in Thai cooking. Often used in place of ginger.

garam masala A northern Indian spice mix which means 'warming spice mix', it mostly contains coriander, cumin, cardamom, black pepper, cloves, cinnamon and nutmeg. There are many versions and you can buy ready-ground mixes or make your own (page 36).

ghee A highly clarified butter made from cow or water buffalo milk. Ghee can be heated to a high temperature without burning and has an aromatic flavour. Vegetable ghees are also available but don't have the same aromatic qualities. You can substitute clarified butter, or make your own ghee by melting unsalted butter in a saucepan, bringing to a simmer and cooking for about 30 minutes to evaporate out any water. Skim any scum off the surface, then drain the ghee off, leaving the white sediment behind. Leave to cool.

ginger Fresh young ginger should have a smooth, pinkish beige skin and be firm and juicy. As it ages, the skin toughens and the flesh becomes more fibrous. Avoid old ginger which is wrinkled as it will be tough. Choose pieces you can snap easily. Ginger is measured in centimetre or inch pieces and this means pieces with an average-sized width. Ginger is also available dried and ground.

Indian bay leaves (cassia leaves) The dried leaves of the cassia tree. They look a little like dried European bay leaves, but have a cinnamon flavour.

jaggery Made from sugar cane, this is a raw sugar with a caramel flavour and alcoholic aroma. Jaggery, which is sold in lumps, is slightly sticky and varies in colour depending on the juice from which it is made. Jaggery can also refer to palm sugar. Soft brown sugar can be used as a substitute.

kaffir limes (makruts) These knobbly skinned fruit are used for their zest rather than their bitter juice. Leaves are double leaves with a fragrant citrus oil. They are used very finely shredded or torn into large pieces. Available fresh or frozen.

karhai/kadhai A deep wok-shaped cooking dish used in Indian cookery. Heavy cast iron ones are best for deep-frying and carbon steel ones for frying.

kecap manis A thick, sweet soy sauce used as a flavouring.

lemongrass The fibrous stalk of a citrus perfumed grass, it is finely chopped or sliced or cut into chunks. Discard the outer layers until you reach a softer pink layer.

maida Plain white flour used in naan and other Indian recipes. Plain (all-purpose) flour is a suitable substitute.

mustard seeds Yellow, brown and black mustard seeds are used in Indian cooking. Brown and black are interchangeable. The seeds are either added to hot oil to pop, to make them taste nutty rather than hot, or are ground to a paste before use in which case they are still hot. Split mustard seeds are called mustard dal.

okra Also known as ladies' fingers, these are green, fuzzy, tapered pods with ridges running down them. When cut they give off a glue like substance which disappears during cooking.

palm sugar Is made by boiling sugar palm sap until it turns into a granular paste. Sold in hard cakes of varying sizes or as a slightly softer version in tubs. Unrefined, soft light brown sugar can be used instead.

panch phoron Meaning five spices, Panch Poran contains fennel, brown mustard, nigella seeds, fenugreek, and cumin seeds in equal amounts.

paprika A reddish orange powder made from ground capsicums (peppers). It is sweet rather than hot, and used for colour. It needs to be fried before use.

peppercorns Green peppercorns are used fresh in curries. Dried white pep-percorns are used as a seasoning in dishes and as a garnish but black pep-per is seldom used in curries.

pine nuts Small cream-coloured seeds from Neosia pine cones which grow in the Himalayas. They can be used both whole and ground.

pomegranate seeds Used whole or ground to add a sour, tangy flavour to dishes. Buy from Indian food shops.

poppadom These are quite thin wafers made from a paste of lentil (gram) flours, rice flour or even tapioca or sago flour, which is rolled out very thin and then sun-dried. To fry poppadoms,

heat about 2.5 cm (1 inch) oil in a frying pan until very hot, add poppadoms one at a time and press down into oil with a spatula until they expand and lighten.

poppy seeds In India, white poppy seeds are used rather than European black or grey ones. They are used either whole or ground. Don't use black poppy seeds as a thickener or the colour of your dish will be greyish.

red Asian shallots Small reddish-purple shallots used in Southeast Asia. French shallots can be used instead.

rice flour Finely ground rice used for making dosas. A coarser grind called idli-rava is used for idlis.

saffron strands These strands give an intense yellow colour and musky aroma. Only a few are needed for each dish. Soak in liquid before use.

sesame oil A strongly flavoured oil extracted from roasted sesame seeds, it should be used sparingly.

shrimp paste Very pungent pulverised shrimp. Refrigerate after opening.

snake (yard long) beans Sold in coils or bunches. Eaten fresh and cooked. Green beans can be used instead.

split peas Split dried peas which need

to be soaked before they are cooked and have a slightly chewy texture. Green and yellow ones are available.

tamarind A souring agent made from the pods of the tamarind tree. Sold either as a block of pulp, as fibrous husk and seeds, as cleaned pulp, or as tamarind purée or concentrate.

tandoori food colouring A bright red powder used to colour tandoori dishes. Add to tandoori pastes to colour them.

tava A specially shaped hotplate used in India to cook breads. Some are flat, others are slightly convex or concave. Keep oiled to stop them going rusty.

Thai basil Has purplish stems, green leaves and an aniseed aroma and flavour.

toor dal Also called yellow lentils, these come oiled and plain. Oiled ones look greasy and need to be soaked in hot water to remove the oil. Soak dal for a few hours before cooking.

turmeric Dried turmeric, sold whole or ground, is a deep yellow colour. It has a slightly bitter flavour and a pungent aroma. Turmeric is used for both colour and flavour.

vinegar Made from fermented alcohol, vinegars based on sugar cane molasses (dark) and coconut (clear) are used, mainly in Parsi, Anglo-Indian and Goan food. If unavailable, substitute balsamic or white vinegar.

yoghurt Yoghurt in India is made with whole milk and is a thick, set yoghurt.

INDEX